# CONFESSION

# CONFESSION

*Five Sentences*
*That Will Heal Your Life*

DR. TOM CURRAN

WITH

TRACEY ROCKWELL

MCF PRESS

Printed in the United States of America by MCF Press, P.O. Box 24886, Federal Way, WA 98093. No part of this book may be used or reproduced in any manner whatsoever without written permission except in the case of brief quotations embodied in critical articles or reviews.

Cover design by Jonny Georgeson and John Anderson

Cover photograph by Jonny Georgeson

Painting of the face of Jesus on the front cover
by Tracy L. Christianson

Library of Congress Number: 2010921437

ISBN: 0-9817145-2-8

ISBN: 978-0-9817145-2-3

OTHER BOOKS BY DR. TOM CURRAN

*The Mass: Four Encounters With Jesus
That Will Change Your Life*

# ACKNOWLEDGEMENTS

*Tom:* To Kari and my kids, Mary Grace, Anne Marie, Mary Catherine, Arianna, John Mark, John Luke, Annelise and "the baby in mommy's tummy": thank you for being willing to join me in making lots of sacrifices of time together because "Daddy is still working on his book." Kids, I owe you lots of play time and I look forward to paying that debt. Kari, you are such a gift to me.

To Tracey: you have been the engine that kept this book going forward. Your organizing, structuring, editing and help with the writing have been essential in completing the book. Without you, this book does not exist.

*Tracey:* Thank you to the staff at MyCatholicFaith.org for their ongoing support and encouragement. To Jonny Georgeson who labored through many drafts of our cover, to John Anderson for helping with that project, to Suzanne for your marketing efforts and to Father Tom Vandenberg, thank you. To Lori, thank you for your steady, firm guidance in all the work of the ministry office. To my husband Joe, and my children Joseph, Jordan and Lauren, thank you for the joy you bring every day. Finally to Tom Curran, who, through his faithful submission of his considerable gifts to God, has awakened and renewed a love for Jesus Christ and for our Catholic faith in so many people, including me, thank you for your generosity in allowing me to do what I love for the glory of God.

# CONTENTS

[I]t is necessary that in [Confession]
there should be a pronouncement by the individual
himself with the whole depth of his conscience
and
with the whole of his sense of guilt and of trust in God,
placing himself like the Psalmist before God to confess:
*"Against you...have I sinned"*.
In faithfully observing the centuries-old practice of the
Sacrament of Penance—
the practice of individual confession,
*with a personal act of sorrow*
*and the intention to amend and make satisfaction*
the Church is therefore defending the human soul's
individual right:
*man's right to a more personal encounter with the*
*crucified forgiving Christ,*
with Christ saying, through the minister of
the sacrament of Reconciliation:
"Your sins are forgiven";
*"Go, and do not sin again"*
As is evident, this is also a right on Christ's part
with regard to every human being redeemed by him:
his right to meet each one of us in that key moment
in the soul's life constituted by the moment of
conversion and forgiveness.

Pope John Paul II, *Redemptor hominis* 20
*(emphasis added)*

# PART I

# ON YOUR MARK

# RUN, DON'T WALK

In more than two decades of serving the Catholic Church as a layman, catechist and theologian, I have met many Catholics who go to Mass faithfully and try to honor God in how they live, but who don't feel the need to go to Confession regularly, if at all. Absent from their awareness is the idea that going to Confession frequently is a critical, necessary aid in striving to fulfill God's call for their lives. I'm not saying these Catholics have rejected Confession. Rather, they have just drifted away from the practice of the sacrament. Then there are those Catholics who run from the sacrament—who avoid it like the plague.

If you go to Confession infrequently, you probably haven't experienced the sacrament as an important part of your relationship with God. When I say "infrequently" I mean once a year as part of your "Easter duty," or only when you commit a "big sin." If this describes you, keep reading. You will be amazed to discover what you have been missing. Once you really understand what is happening in Confession, you will begin to seek regularly what you have been avoiding.

For a period in my life, I avoided Confession like the plague. Now I wouldn't miss it for the world. What happened? I discovered that Confession is precisely the place I need to run to when I am infected with a plague, a spiritual disease called sin. Sin wreaks havoc on our spiritual health, like a disease does to our bodies. Confession is God's cure for the spiritual illnesses that ail us, weigh us down and hold us back. If we are suffering from bronchitis or a chest infection, we do not hesitate to go to the doctor for antibiotics to clear up the illness. Yet we shy away from going to Confession to clear up the sin that infects our lives, weakens our wills and clouds our intellects. Our natural reticence to bring out into the open those places in our lives where we've dishonored God doesn't help matters. When we are ashamed of something we've done, we would rather hide or hold it inside than bring it out in Confession.

Once I experienced the healing power of the sacrament, I realized the frightening thing was not *going to* Confession, but *missing* Confession. Confession is not irrelevant to my spiritual condition—the priest, the confessional and Confession are as relevant to my spiritual health as a doctor, hospital and medicine are to my physical health.

Unfortunately, there have not been sufficient rescue efforts to seek out those who have wandered away from, or who consciously flee, Confession. If the practice of Confession has been absent from your life for a significant time, please believe me when I say that you are headed towards a dangerous precipice. Consider this book a light, a rescue beacon for you and/or others you know who have meandered away or who have sprinted from the safe haven of Confession.

I wrote my first book, *The Mass: Four Encounters with Jesus that will Change Your Life,* because so many Catholics go to Mass out of obligation and end up distracted and bored. My challenge there was to help Catholics see the Mass with new eyes, to recognize Jesus Christ Who approaches us at Mass in four distinct ways, so that our lives can be changed. Here my challenge is different. Most Catholics don't go to Confession often enough for it to become boring to them. In fact, boring is probably the last word a typical Catholic would associate with Confession. Other words that come to mind are *frightening* (for those who are reluctant to reveal the sins they have committed) or *irrelevant* (for those who don't see a need to go to Confession in our modern, enlightened world).

My proposal in this book is a simple one: Catholics who run from Confession, or have simply wandered away, have been swindled. That is what I have seen in more than two decades of helping Catholics grow in faith. What happens when you are swindled? Someone gains your trust and convinces you to give up something valuable in exchange for something less valuable. Worst of all, when you believe the lie of the swindler, you freely, willingly and joyfully give up what is precious because of the expectation of receiving something of greater value in return. Sadly, what you actually get back is worth little, nothing or it may even be harmful.

Furthermore, in the most successful swindles, you don't even realize you have been swindled... you excitedly trade a treasure for trash. You look forward to surrendering a pearl of great price to get a worthless fake in return. Catholics have been told and taught ideas in society, and sadly by some misguided souls in the Church herself, that we don't need to go to Confession, that God understands and sees our good intentions, that God's unconditional love covers all our sins and that Confession is a relic of a bygone age too hung up on guilt and shame. If you bought one of these lines and gave up going to Confession as a result, you have been swindled.

When we ignore or run away from the practice of Confession, we are missing out on an encounter with God that will bring us a peace, freedom and joy this world cannot give and cannot take away. My goal in this book is to restore to you the treasure you may have lost. I will do this by reflecting on five sentences connected with

Confession: *I did it. I am sorry. Forgive me. I will make up for it. I will never do it again.* These sentences are based on the *Acts of the Penitent,* identified in the *Catechism of the Catholic Church* as *contrition, confession, satisfaction* and the act of the priest called *absolution.* The central chapters of the book will explore how each of the sentences relates to the Sacrament of Confession, and how each takes shape in our everyday lives as disciples of Jesus Christ. Tying the five sentences to our everyday living I refer to as "living a confessional life." The concept of living a confessional life dates back to St. Augustine's *Confessions,* but it can be traced all the way back to Jesus Christ crucified, who simultaneously "confesses" the sins of the world (including your sins and mine) and God's love for the world (including God's love for you and me).

Woven through each chapter is teaching about Confession as a sacrament of healing, as it is expressed in the *Catechism of the Catholic Church* and in the writings of *St. Augustine* and *St. Thomas Aquinas,* two of the greatest Doctors of the Catholic Church. Each of the five sentences is connected to the sacrament's healing purpose, as seen most clearly in Chapter Five where I reflect on God's mercy. There we will discover that confessing our sins is never our initiative, but is always a response to God's mercy. It is because of God's mercy that we are drawn home to be reconciled to our heavenly Father through Confession. In the last chapter, *Practice Makes*

*Perfect,* I answer the most commonly asked questions that hold some Catholics back from going to Confession.

If I do my job well, at the end of this book you will be headed in a new direction. Rather than running *from* Confession, (or maybe just ignoring it) you will be running *to* Confession. Why? Because of what awaits you—and even more importantly, because of Who awaits you—in the confessional, Jesus Christ Himself. He is there at work in every Confession, as the Divine Physician, to bring spiritual healing to your life. Chapter by chapter you will grow in your desire to live a confessional life, and to make a good Confession a regular part of your life of faith as a Catholic. So please join me in stepping up to the starting line. Get loose and ready to run. On your mark, get set... let's go!

# CHAPTER ONE

# RECOGNITION: I AM BLIND AND DEAF

*You called me; you cried aloud to me;*
*you broke my barrier of deafness.*
*You shone upon me;*
*your radiance enveloped me;*
*you put my blindness to flight.*

St. Augustine, *Confessions*

Early one brisk January evening a couple of years ago, I was driving to a speaking engagement at a parish in North Seattle. As I exited the highway I noticed a coffee shop on the other side of the road. A good, hot cup of coffee was exactly what I needed, so I parked, went in and ordered an extra hot mocha. As the barista was steaming milk and preparing the espresso, my eyes were drawn to an odd sight happening outside in the parking lot on the far side of the coffee shop. A man about my age wearing a jacket and a backpack was slowly walking forward with both his arms extended in front of him, as if he were walking in the dark, even though there was still daylight. He bumped into a parked car, steadied himself with his hands, changed direction and then almost immediately bumped into another car.

I went outside to find out what was going on. As I approached the man I saw a large round button pinned to his jacket that read, "I am blind and deaf." That explained his outstretched arms and bumping into cars. This guy needed help, and I wanted to help him, but I was at a loss. How do I communicate with someone who is blind and deaf? Ordinary modes of communication won't work. After thinking about it for a moment, I did the only thing that seemed to make any sense; slowly I reached out my hand and touched him on the shoulder. He flinched at my touch, since I had startled him. But he quickly composed himself and extended his left arm toward me almost like he wanted to shake hands, but with the palm of his hand turned up and his fingers together. He then used the pointer finger of his right hand to mimic the act of writing on the palm of his outstretched left hand. It wasn't hard to figure out that he was showing me how we could communicate: through touch. He reached out his hand towards me and I put my hand in his. Slowly but surely, he began writing letters in my hand, letters that spelled a word, and then more letters that became more words. Words connected into a meaningful sentence. When I understood what he was asking or saying, it was my turn to take his hand and reply by writing my own string of letters and words in his palm until they made a sentence. It felt more than a bit awkward, but regardless, by putting my hand into his and taking his hand into mine, we could overcome his blindness and deafness. Touch was a way for us to communicate.

What I learned from all this back and forth writing in each other's hands was that he was trying to get home. So I wrote in the palm of his hand, "Do you need a ride?" He nodded. With that cue, I took his arm and guided him over to my car and into the front passenger's seat, got back in the driver's seat and buckled myself in. I noticed that my new traveling companion had a notebook out on his lap and he was writing in it. This man who could not see or hear had learned to write! He wrote that his name was Brian. I traced my first name into his palm. He nodded and then wrote down the address where he wanted me to drive him; it was an intersection about a mile from where we were parked. I started the car and turned down the road towards his destination. Along the drive, he explained how he had come to be at the coffee shop. He wrote that he had a full-time job in a city fifty miles south of Seattle, and had arranged to have a shuttle van drive him back and forth to work during the week. The shuttle picked him up and dropped him off at the corner where the coffee shop was located. He had arranged for a taxi to pick him up there after work and drive him the rest of the way home. For whatever reason, that day the taxi didn't show up. Needing a ride, he had tried to make his way over to the coffee shop to ask someone to call him a taxi. That explained why I saw him bumping into parked cars. This evening, I got to be his taxi.

We arrived at the destination he had written in his notebook. He asked if I could help him out of the car and orient him in the right direction on the sidewalk. Once there, he could make it the rest of the way home on his own. Of course I agreed to help, but before I could get out of the car, he reached over and felt down next to my seat where my seatbelt was inserted into the buckle. He was confirming that I had driven with my seatbelt fastened. For the second to last time, he took his pen and wrote something in his notebook, "Why didn't you put on my seatbelt?" I sat there stunned. When I first got in the car with Brian I thought about fastening his seatbelt, but I didn't. Why not? Because it was uncomfortable. That was the only reason. I didn't feel comfortable reaching across this unknown person and buckling him in. I never even considered the situation I put Brian in; 'uncomfortable' doesn't begin to describe it. What would it be like to be driven in a car without being buckled in a seatbelt, when you couldn't see or hear? Think about it. You wouldn't know when the car was going to slow down or speed up, turn or go straight. The simple act of buckling Brian in would have eliminated much of his concern, but I had failed him. I wrote in his hand, "I am sorry. Please forgive me." He wrote the last message to me in his notebook, a message of mercy: "I forgive you." I helped Brian get in the right position on the sidewalk. He nodded thanks to me for my help, took out his walking stick and headed home.

Driving away from Brian, I couldn't help but be moved by what had just happened. Beyond my sense of shame about not buckling Brian's seatbelt, I was deeply convicted about something else, something that made me feel like I should be wearing the button on Brian's jacket that said, "I am blind and deaf." God had given me the incredible abilities of seeing and hearing, and truth be told, I took them for granted. When was the last time I thanked God, *really* thanked God, for the ability to see and hear? I couldn't remember. After meeting Brian, how could I ever forget to thank God for these gifts? God used Brian to teach me gratitude. But God was teaching me so much more through my encounter with him.

## PUTTING MYSELF IN GOD'S HANDS

When I met Brian I was on my way to an event where I would teach others about the Catholic faith. That evening, Brian did more than teach me about faith, he was a living witness about what it means to have faith. What did Brian do that expressed the essence of faith? He put himself completely in my hands. Brian is a man who has to rely on a taxi and a shuttle to drive him a hundred miles or more just so he can get to work and back. All by itself, that is impressive. But more than that, in so many aspects of his life, Brian willingly puts himself completely in the hands of others, even strangers like me, for the most basic of necessities. The evening of our providential meeting, he trusted me completely without even knowing my name, just so he could get home! Unfortunately, his faith in me wasn't entirely warranted, since I couldn't even be trusted to buckle him in. Brian is a man who lives out the most important and profound meaning of faith, the act of completely *entrusting* oneself (*surrendering* and *abandoning* are other words used in our Catholic tradition) into the hands of God. What was so astonishing to me was that he wasn't putting himself into the hands of God. He put himself into my hands!

Sitting in the car alone, I realized something; Brian had trusted me more than I trusted God. His actions that evening expressed a total faith in me even though he had never met me and knew nothing about me. Why didn't I put myself into God's hands as willingly, completely and quickly as Brian put himself into mine? I wasn't blind and deaf regarding God. Or was I? I didn't think so. Then why would I hesitate to entrust myself completely into God's

hands? Didn't I believe that God loved me enough to seek
me out when I was bumping around the parking lot of
my life, to find a way to communicate with me despite my
blindness and deafness and to "buckle me in" and get me
"home" to a safe place? What a gift Brian gave me that
night! What a gift God gave me through Brian that night!
God brought me into contact with a witness to the essence
of faith. I thought I was helping Brian, but Brian helped
me far more. God used a blind and deaf man to reveal
to me that "I am blind and deaf." Blind and deaf to the
ways that God faithfully reaches out to me and touches
me, invites me to take His hand and allow Him to lead me
safely home. Unlike my situation with Brian, God does
not "drop me off" and leave me to make it the rest of the
way home all alone. There is no "I've got it from here" in
my relationship with God. When God leads me home, He
leads me back into His arms like the Prodigal Son, who
comes home to a father who runs out to meet him and
embrace him. Which brings me to Confession.

## THE GIFT OF CONFESSION

Confession is THE Catholic blind spot. "I am blind
and deaf to the blessing of Confession." How many
Catholics could wear that button? Confession is where
God approaches all of us who are blind and deaf to His
faithfulness because of our sin, to offer us His merciful
touch. Through Confession, God safely brings us back

into a loving union with Him in our spiritual home, the Catholic Church. God offers Confession as a gift to Catholics, but like Brian, so many of us are blind and deaf to it in one way or another. Sadly, Brian wakes up each and every day of his life and has no choice but to remain blind and deaf. But we don't! We have a choice. We don't have to remain blind and deaf to the gift of Confession. We can come to understand and experience for ourselves the awesome power of God's mercy that reaches out to us, takes us by the hand and leads us safely home.

I want this book to be a source of renewal for you; a renewal of your ability to see and hear what God makes available to you in the sacrament of Confession. In each chapter we will explore the Catholic Church's teaching on Confession, especially on the meaning of Confession as a sacrament, and then we will connect the act of going to Confession to the rest of your life as a Catholic Christian disciple of Jesus Christ. I am convinced that when you can relate what happens in Confession to your day-to-day experience of living as a disciple, then going to Confession will be something less foreign and disconnected from your life, and more of a condensed expression of how you live as a disciple every day.

# CONFESSION: THE SACRAMENT OF PENANCE AND RECONCILIATION

Let's examine the definition and description of Confession, called the Sacrament of Penance and Reconciliation in the *Catechism of the Catholic Church*. First of all, what is a sacrament? Traditionally understood, sacraments are "effective signs" established by Christ and continued in the Church, signs that communicate the sanctifying grace they signify. For instance, in Baptism we are literally "plunged or immersed" (which is what the word "baptism" means in Greek) in water as the words of Baptism are pronounced over us.

The act of immersing in water is a sign that through this sacrament our entire being is "immersed" in the very life of God. In Baptism, we are filled with God's own life! I become a new creation, an adopted child of God. Being plunged in water or having water poured or sprinkled on us is also an indicator that we are being cleansed or washed clean. Just as we use water to wash up and get clean, using water in Baptism is a sign that this sacrament cleanses us from the stain of sin. How does Baptism accomplish this? Through Jesus Christ. In Baptism, we are immersed in God's life precisely by being plunged into the Pascal Mystery of Jesus Christ's Passion, death and Resurrection. Water is not only a symbol of cleansing, but it is also a symbol of chaos and the powers of death, into which

Jesus Christ is "plunged" through His death on the cross. We could go through each of the sacraments, including the Sacrament of Penance and Reconciliation and take a look at how they are effective signs, but I would like to focus on one aspect of the traditional definition that makes the sacraments, and especially Confession, more personal and meaningful. Sacraments are holy moments where we encounter Jesus Christ. How important is it for us to experience the sacraments as places of encountering Jesus Christ? Read what Pope Benedict XVI stated almost ten years before becoming pope: "If no contact with the living God of all men takes place in the sacraments, then they are empty rituals which tell us nothing nor give us anything."[1]

## HE SEES YOU!

The *Catechism of the Catholic Church* draws attention to this personal, one-to-one encounter aspect of the sacraments by associating the sacraments with an event in the life of Jesus. At the beginning of the Second Part of the *Catechism,* which covers the seven sacraments,

---

1. Ratzinger, Joseph Cardinal. "Relativism: The Central Problem for Faith Today." Address given at the meeting of the Congregation for the Doctrine of the Faith with the presidents of the Doctrinal Commissions of the Bishops' Conferences of Latin America. Guadalajara, Mexico. (May 1996). http://www.ewtn.com/library/CURIA/RATZRELA.htm

there is a page with a fresco of a scene in the Gospel of Mark (Mk 5:25–34) that is meant to express artistically what the *Catechism* is about to state in words about the sacraments. The fresco depicts the encounter of Jesus and the woman with the uncontrollable hemorrhage. In the Gospel story, this woman has been bleeding for twelve years, and because of her bleeding, she was thought of as unclean. To be deemed unclean would have cut her off from the Temple, from Temple worship of God, and from her family and friends. Why? Anyone who touched her or touched anything she touched would be made unclean just as she was unclean. Yet this woman touched Jesus! In the fresco, the woman is shown with her arm outstretched, touching the hem of Jesus' garment. Power flows from Jesus that heals the woman both physically and spiritually. By this action, she is not only made whole in body, but now she is able to be in relationship with God and with her community of faith, family and friends.

In the fresco, only Jesus and the woman are pictured. But that is not the way the event is portrayed in the Scriptures. The Scriptures describe a crowd pressing in on Jesus on every side; He is surrounded by people. When the woman with the flow of blood touches the hem of His garment, He stops and asks, "Who touched me?" as if no one else was even there. This is a crucial aspect of the sacraments: they are places of personal encounter between you and Jesus. Jesus Christ does not see a crowd. He sees you.

## THE SACRAMENTS: A TOUCH THAT RESTORES LIFE

In each of the sacraments, we *encounter* Jesus Christ in a unique way, or at least that's what God intends for us. When I state that we *meet* Him, it's not like a casual meeting between friends or like bumping into someone unexpectedly at the store. In the sacraments, we do not meet Jesus Christ in a vague, diffused way. In each sacramental encounter, Jesus Christ approaches you personally and touches you not at the surface level but in the depths of your heart, in your deepest center. When He touches you He communicates His very life to you in such a profound way that you are transformed into Him! Your humanity is elevated and divinized because Jesus Christ the Redeemer has touched you through the very ritual He established.

You don't have to wonder if this happens only occasionally or only to specially chosen people. He has promised this to all of us in each and every sacramental encounter, and Jesus keeps His promises. If I ever miss out on this personal transformative encounter that sets me free, it isn't because Jesus Christ didn't approach me. Rather, it is because "I am blind and deaf" through my lack of faith or my sinfulness, and end up cutting myself off from what Jesus Christ offered me. Jesus Christ the

Redeemer reaches out to touch our lives in the sacraments. When the Redeemer touches us, redemption touches our lives. In the sacraments, Jesus breaks our enslavement to sin and grants us the freedom that comes with being a child of God. Along with this freedom He grants us a type of peace and joy that this world cannot give or take away.

It's true that with the eyes of faith you can come to see God in the world around you, and encounter Christ in the events and people you meet each day. But encounters with Jesus Christ in the sacraments are unique. Jesus established them as promised places of special encounters with Him, encounters that redeem, save, heal, transform and set free. But there are seven different sacraments; does the Catholic Church distinguish any particular ways that Christ's redemptive encounter is at work in the various sacraments? The answer is yes!

## TAKE YOUR MEDICINE!

St. Thomas Aquinas, in his *Summa Theologica*, proposed that we can relate the grace given in the sacraments to different events, stages or aspects of life in this world. You can probably guess some of the connections he makes. He associates Baptism with coming to birth, Confirmation with the ritual acknowledgement of arriving at adulthood, the Eucharist with nourishment and growth, marriage with the act of reproduction in nature, the priesthood with governance, and Extreme Unction (what we call today the Anointing of the Sick) with the moment of departing this earth.

What about Confession? In his writings, St. Thomas associates Confession with medicine that restores health. Just as we use medicine to help us recover from physical sickness, in our spiritual lives we are to use the sacrament of Confession to help us recover from the sickness of the soul that sin inflicts.

I don't like being sick. I don't think anyone does. Every winter, the flu makes its visit to the Curran household. It's not a pretty sight: fevers, coughing, body aches, congestion, dizziness, nausea, low energy. Sometimes when I'm really sick, I don't remember what it feels like to be healthy, and I can't imagine a time when I will be healthy again. Being sick in the body is awful and, like most people, I have no fear and no qualms about using medicine to help me feel well and to recover my health.

Sin impacts us like a bad flu, or worse, a deadly disease. It makes us sick at heart or spiritually sick. There are lots of symptoms of spiritual sickness: fear, confusion, spiritual bondage, disgust at oneself, aversion to spiritual things and low energy for spiritual activities, to name a few. Sometimes, when I am seriously sick in my soul, I can't remember God's loving kindness towards me and I can't imagine that God would want to show me favor or free me from my miserable condition. The good news is that He does want me free from spiritual sickness and He provides the medicine: Confession. That is our heavenly medicine. I don't know anyone who wants to stay spiritually sick. Then why do we avoid Confession? What awaits us is medicine for our souls.

## A SACRAMENT OF HEALING

While referencing St. Thomas Aquinas' association of "the stages of natural life and the stages of the spiritual life," the *Catechism of the Catholic Church* uses a different manner of sorting the seven sacraments. It divides the sacraments into three categories: initiation, vocation and healing. The sacraments of initiation are Baptism, Confirmation and Holy Communion. They "initiate" or "incorporate" us into the Church (i.e. make us members of the Church). The sacraments of vocation are Holy Matrimony and Holy Orders. The *Catechism* calls these sacraments "at the service of communion" since they are God given means by which some are called to serve others in their growth in holiness. Lastly, there are the sacraments of healing: Anointing of the Sick and Confession.

The Anointing of the Sick is sometimes called The Sacrament of the Sick because it is offered to those who are sick in their bodies. Depending on the circumstances, the Anointing of the Sick includes prayers for the healing of the sick person and for the restoration of bodily health. What about Confession? Confession is a sacrament that brings healing to the soul. Through God's mercy, the penitent (the person who is confessing) experiences a "spiritual resurrection." Not only sick souls, but spiritually dead souls are brought back to life in Confession!

Think about that for a minute. The Catholic Church has always taught that Confession, or the Sacrament of Penance and Reconciliation, is best understood through the concept of healing. Whether you read St. Thomas Aquinas or the *Catechism*, you see a common theme: Confession is a Christ-established event where He has promised to meet us with His healing power. If the words "healing" or "place of healing" or "healing encounter" do not spring immediately to mind when you think of going to Confession, then you misunderstand what it is all about. Read one last quote about this theme from the *Catechism* regarding the encounter with Jesus Christ in Confession:

> Christ is at work in each of the sacraments. He personally addresses every sinner: "My son, your sins are forgiven." He is the physician tending each one of the sick who need him to cure them. He raises them up and reintegrates them into fraternal communion. (CCC 1484)

## MEETING IN AN UNLIKELY PLACE

Like the other sacraments, there are certain qualifications necessary to be an acceptable candidate for

Confession. For example, in order to receive the Anointing of the Sick, you have to be seriously sick. Have you ever thought about the qualifications you need to be able to go to Confession? The answer is striking: I need to be a person who has betrayed Jesus Christ. For me to encounter Christ's special touch of spiritual healing, I have to fail Him. Jesus said, "Those who are well do not need a physician, but the sick do. I did not come to call the righteous but sinners"(Mk. 2:17). It is the opposite of what we expect. Remember, the seven sacraments are seven rites established by Jesus Christ where He has *promised* to meet us. I don't know about you, but when I promise to meet someone, it's not going to be in that place where they have betrayed me, failed me, denied me, run from me and jumped into a place of their own destruction. I'm not going to promise to meet someone there, unless it is to punish them. It's a good thing I'm not God!

We will never stop being amazed at how "God's ways are not our ways" (Isaiah 55:8). But Jesus Christ is God. And He *has* promised to meet you in those hidden places in your life where you have failed Him and where you now suffer the consequences. This is a stunning truth. "Where you have failed me, I promise to meet you." It's as if Jesus is saying to you, "When you are blind and deaf and bumping around because of your spiritual sickness, I will seek you out, reach out and touch you, take you by the hand and lead you safely home to my Father, where you will be healed, restored and set free." When an ordained priest sits in his confessional he is a "sign," a representative of Jesus Christ, waiting for you to come and acknowledge, "That's me with the big button on my jacket. I am blind and deaf. Please heal me."

## LIVING A CONFESSIONAL LIFE

One of the biggest reasons why many Catholics go to Confession so rarely is because we don't see how it connects with our daily life of faith. We go to Confession when we have to and then leave it behind until the next time we have to go again. Not much of a connection there! The reality of Confession does not obviously connect to our day-to-day lives, at least that's what we think. This is another example of how blind and deaf we can be to something that was profoundly obvious to many of the great saints, like St. Augustine.

St. Augustine is probably best known for his autobiographical work, *Confessions*. It is commonly thought that this book is St. Augustine's account of his long journey to faith in God that "confesses" in great detail all his horrific sins. If that is all you've heard, then you've missed out on the essence of what *Confessions* is all about. Yes, the central purpose of *Confessions* is to confess, but Augustine's primary purpose is to make a confession of faith in God, a confession that takes two expressions. First of all, it is a confession of God's glory, and second it is a confession of his sinfulness. For Augustine, it is essential to connect the confessing of one's sins to the confessing of God's glory. It is only in the light of God's majesty that I will truly recognize my deep misery. Divine holiness and human sinfulness are confessed together, like holding up a coin and acknowledging its two sides. What do I mean? Let me give you an example.

At Mass we gather together in God's holy presence and we confess our sins: I confess to Almighty God... What follows immediately after? A confession of God's glory: Glory to God in the highest! The *Catechism* also mentions this dual aspect of Confession in its teaching on the Sacrament of Penance and Reconciliation:

> It is called the *sacrament of confession*, since the disclosure or confession of sins to a priest is an essential element of this sacrament. In a profound sense it is also a "confession"—acknowledgment and praise—of the holiness of God and of his mercy toward sinful man. (CCC 1424)

*Ad maiorem Dei gloriam* (For the greater Glory of God!) was the motto of St. Ignatius Loyola, the founder of the Jesuits. Every day, the goal of all he thought, said and did was to glorify God, to "confess" to the world that God is glorious. Confession refers to so much more than the Sacrament of Penance and Reconciliation. Confession can be a lens through which we see the whole of our lives as disciples of Jesus Christ. Our Catholic tradition puts it like this: our lives should be a confession of our faith *(confessio fidei)* in God. Living as a disciple of Jesus Christ is living a life that confesses God's glory *(confessio gloriae)* and my sinfulness *(confessio peccati)*—a life that confesses God's greatness and my littleness. Your life confesses something. The question is, how clearly, how profoundly, is your life confessing *who* you really are and *whose* you really are?

## WHAT IS YOUR LIFE CONFESSING?

Let's revisit for a moment the fresco of the woman with the flow of blood in the *Catechism*. She is a beautiful example of living a confessional life. The woman knew that she was unclean and felt deeply the ramifications of this uncleanness. She couldn't hide her condition. Her own body "confessed" to herself and everyone that knew her what her standing was before God. Yet she reached out despite her personal situation. Reaching out for the hem of Jesus' garment was her "confession of faith" in His power, His ability and His willingness to address her physical malady and unclean status. When power flows forth from Him and she is healed, her healing "confesses God's glory." She herself becomes a manifestation of God's glorious will to heal and set free. In this encounter, Jesus Christ acts on her behalf as her personal Redeemer; she is set free inside and out, physically and spiritually. Her confessional life is a model for what happens in the sacraments and especially in Confession. Our confession of faith leads us to confess our sins through which God's will to save is made manifest and God is glorified.

If Confession remains something that we do reluctantly once a year in accord with the law of the Church, or think is relevant only when we commit mortal sins, then we are missing out on the way that Confession can be linked to living a confessional life. What are you confessing by the way you live your life?

THE FIVE SENTENCES

The more we see ourselves called to live a confessional life, the more natural and even attractive it will be to go to Confession. I mentioned in the Introduction that we would be reflecting on the *Acts of the Penitent* as defined in the *Catechism of the Catholic Church,* and linking them to our everyday lives. What would that look like? Let me give you an example. My wife Kari and I have taught our children that when they fight or offend one another, they must reconcile or make up. We have taught them five sentences that express what we expect of them when they hurt each other, sentences drawn from what we do in Confession. Ask any of my kids, down to my three-year-old, "What do you say when you get in a fight and have to make up with your brother or sister?" They will look at you and say, "I did it. I am sorry. Forgive me. I will make up for it. And I will never do it again." Those sentences unpack what happens in Confession. Those sentences also blossom into a confessional life. We're trying to teach our kids the meaning and reality of living a confessional life from an early age. But it's never too late to get started. My hope is that this book will connect Confession to *your* life. When that happens, your life will naturally lead you to Confession, and you will follow willingly. Christ is waiting to heal me? Who wants to miss out on all that spiritual healing? Not me. And I bet you don't either.

---

# CHAPTER TWO

# PRESCRIPTION: BE HEALED!

*Confession heals,*
*confession justifies,*
*confession grants pardon of sin.*
*All hope consists in confession.*
*In confession there is a chance for mercy.*
*Believe it firmly.*
*Do not doubt,*
*do not hesitate,*
*never despair of the mercy of God.*
*Hope and have confidence in confession.*

St. Isidore of Seville

Did I really do that? Yes, I did. It's been almost ten years, but I still remember it clearly. One summer evening, I got out my lawn mower to perform the weekly chore of cutting the grass. For me, it was simply that—a chore. Not everyone is like me. Some people love working outside in the yard; my wife Kari is one of them. Being outside in beautiful weather, getting her hands and knees dirty tending flowers; what could be better? The smell of freshly cut grass and the look of a manicured lawn make even mowing the lawn appealing to her. I'm not there.

Without paying much attention I went through the motions of taking out the lawnmower, filling it with gas, attaching the grass catcher, pulling the cord to start it, and then pushing the mower along the same pattern I followed every time: back and forth, back and forth, in neat lines. About halfway through the yard, I spotted something lying across the lawn. The garden hose.

Kari loves planting flowers in big pots, in hanging baskets and in strategic places around the backyard. She does a beautiful job. But taking care of those flowers requires regular watering, thus the need for the long garden hose. On this particular day, Kari hadn't wound up the hose. As my mower got closer to the hose I asked myself, "Do I really need to take the extra 10 seconds to move the hose? I don't think the lawnmower will hit it. It looks like it is low enough in the grass for the mower to pass over it." From deep inside my lazy, disengaged soul came the answer, "The lawnmower will clear the hose!" I discovered the disappointing truth a few seconds later when *WHAP!* The blade sliced into the hose, stalling the lawnmower.

## A VENIAL GASH

Many of you reading the book must be saying, "You're not serious, are you? Did this really happen?" Yes, it happened. I really did it. Backing the mower off the hose, I examined the damage I'd done, only to discover a great big gash in the hose. When I turned on the water, a good bit of it leaked out of the gash I'd made, though some water continued down and out the end of the hose. It took several strips of duct tape to repair the hose, though it still leaked a bit. Worse still was admitting to Kari what I had done. I was reluctant, but when I finally did, her response was "You did WHAT? You have got to be kidding me!" It was embarrassing to reveal my lack of engagement and laziness and to take responsibility for the consequences of my lack of care.

In theological terms, I was responsible for causing a *venial* gash in the hose. It could have been worse. My mower could have cut all the way through the hose. That would have been a *mortal* gash, since then no water would reach the end of the hose. If the damage wasn't repaired, the flowers, cut off from life-giving water, were as good as dead.

## DOING MY CHORES

I grew up Catholic, and when it came to Confession it was mostly a chore, sometimes even literally so. Every month or two, the list of Saturday chores prepared by my mom or dad would have on it both "Mow the lawn" and "Go to Confession." Two chores. Growing up, these were two required activities that were more alike in my mind than I want to admit.

Confession was mostly taught to me as a requirement when I committed a mortal sin. I remember learning the difference between mortal and venial sins and discovering that mortal sin was deadly to my soul.[1] I didn't know exactly what that meant, but it was clear to me that my mortal sins needed to be dealt with by going to Confession. Committing a mortal sin cut me off completely from the flow of the Living Water, the Holy Spirit, in my soul. Confession was the God-given means of restoring the flow, like the duct tape for my hose, only it worked perfectly! Of course, I was taught that venial sins were still bad and to be avoided because every sin broke God's law and was deserving of punishment. If mortal sins completely cut me off from communion with God, each venial sin was like a small gash that diminished the flow of God's life in me.

---

1. Mortal sin involves a serious, weighty matter (e.g. the Ten Commandments) and it also involves our knowledge and our will. When I have full knowledge that what I am doing is seriously wrong and still fully choose to do it, then I commit a mortal sin. Venial sins fall short in one of those three aspects of sin, so that it's either not a serious matter, or I lack full knowledge or full consent when I act.

Unfortunately this fostered in me a way of seeing Confession as a chore and an unavoidable and unloved requirement. Confessing what I had done to Kari was not enjoyable at all. I would much rather avoid admitting to embarrassing personal failures, and for me that was what Confession was all about. I never associated the idea of Confession with healing or with having a life-restoring encounter with Jesus Christ, my forgiving Lord.

## AN APPOINTMENT WITH YOUR DIVINE PHYSICIAN

What would have helped me was another way of seeing Confession. If only I had been able to connect going to Confession with going to a doctor's office when I was sick. I may not want to tell the doctor what's going on with me, but I'm smart enough to know if I don't, I won't get the treatment I need to be cured. My condition might get worse. Being sick has many effects on my body, and the worse the effects, the more likely I'll get to the doctor as quickly as I can. What I would *not* do is run from the doctor's office.

Confession is your doctor's office. Your divine physician Jesus Christ is at work in His ordained son, the priest, waiting to restore you to health. St. Augustine taught that only what was revealed would be healed. If I do not reveal my spiritual sickness, then the effects of those sins will only get worse. But what are the effects of sin? Maybe if we had a better understanding of the impact of sin on our lives we would move away from seeing Confession as an unavoidable requirement that we run from, to an appointment with our Divine Physician that we run to.

## EFFECTS OF SIN ON OUR LIVES

What are the symptoms of our spiritual sickness and the effects of sin, even venial sins, on our lives? The traditional way of summing up the impact or effect of any sin on our lives is as follows: *sin darkens our intellect, weakens our will, disorders our passions* and *increases concupiscence.* What does that mean?

*Sin darkens the intellect.* To have a darkened intellect means that the truths of faith I used to see so clearly, accept so readily and experience so profoundly become diminished, obscured and confused in my mind. Believing that God exists, loves me and has a plan for my life is so important. When I sin, it impacts how deeply these truths live in me. If I lose my grip on that truth, then other ideas and falsehoods will begin to confuse and cloud my thinking. I find myself asking things like, "Does God really love me? I have done such hateful things. Why would God want to have anything to do with me? Does God even exist at all?" That's what happens to our minds when we sin. That's not all; sin wreaks havoc on other aspects of our lives as well.

*Sin weakens the will.* To have a weakened will means that in the face of a decision to do something virtuous or godly or to avoid something evil, we find ourselves lacking the capability to *will* to do what we want. St. Paul dramatically describes his experience of being a slave to sin in his letter to the Romans:

> What I do, I do not understand. For I do not do what I want, but I do what I hate...So now it is no longer I who do it, but sin that dwells in me. For I know that good does not dwell in me, that is, in my flesh. The *willing* is ready at hand, but *doing* the good is not. For I do not do the good I want, but I do the evil I do not want. Now if (I) do what I do not want, it is no longer I who do it, but sin that dwells in me. (Rom 7:15, 17–20) *(emphasis mine)*

Choosing to sin, even once, saps us of some of the strength we need to resist that same sin the next time we are tempted by it. Choosing to sin weakens our capacity to say "no" to sin and our ability to say "yes" to God. That's why St. Paul uses the image of slavery when discussing sin. Committing a particular sin eventually becomes a habit, making me a slave to it. I end up in bondage to sin the way slaves are shackled, with no escape by my own power. My will is too weak. I certainly didn't plan on, expect or want the slavery to sin I experience.

Sin has an addictive quality, and over time it leaves us powerless before it, whatever *it* is (e.g. internet pornography, gossip, anger, envy, pride, greed, etc.). What we have done is freely chosen to gradually destroy our freedom to say no to sin, one choice at a time. That's what is meant by sin weakens our wills.

*Sin disorders the passions.* When you read the word *passions* think *appetites* or *desires.* What do I hunger for? What pulls me toward it? What do I desire? When I live a holy life, my passions are in peaceful harmony, all of them urging me to God or to do what honors God. When I sin, the tranquil ordering of desires is disturbed, like a rock being thrown into a still, calm pond. Sin sends ripples into my passions, creating a wave that would carry me away from God or from what honors God if I chose to act on it. We experience this in daily life all the time; I desire to be healthy and I desire to eat chocolate cake. Both desires live in me, but not peacefully! I see the beauty of God's creation in that attractive woman and I desire that woman in lustful ways. Both desires are pulling at me; one honors God and the other doesn't. I desire to celebrate my good friend's success and I am envious over what she has and I am secretly jealous of it. The conflict of desires. We all know it. Committing a sin, even a venial sin, increases the disturbance of the desires that live in us, making us lack the harmony, order and peace that God intends for our lives.

*Sin increases concupiscence.* Concupiscence is a fancy term referring to the urge toward sin that results from sin. The *Catechism of the Catholic Church* also refers to concupiscence as the tinder (or igniter or kindling) for sin (1264). Sin is extremely combustible, and we are putting our spiritual lives in danger when we give in to sin. It's not safe to play fast and loose with any sin. They just might explode in ways that damage ourselves and others, especially those nearest and dearest to us. This is so true and so obvious that it's amazing we settle for sin so easily. Think of any of the seven deadly sins and see how giving in to any one of them not only increases the urge toward that sin, but how much weaker our resistance becomes to that sin's explosive character. Anger is the clearest example. Are you or someone you know prone to anger? Give in to anger today and tomorrow and watch how quickly you end up with explosive flare-ups of anger in situations with loved ones where anger was not warranted whatsoever. Concupiscence is an effect of sin that must not be ignored.

## HEALING THE GASH

Are you convinced yet? Any sin, including venial sin, is a spiritual disease that devastates the soul. It needs to be addressed right now, with courage and conviction, before things get worse! The best news of all is that Jesus Christ, our Divine Physician, has provided us with Confession as a place where He will minister His cure for our deadly disease and all its effects. Confession is not just a *requirement* in cases of mortal sin but an incredible *remedy* for the effects of each and every sin. Just as sinning has its effects, going to Confession also has its effects.

A good Confession brings God's healing power into our lives as a remedy for the evil effects of every sin we confess. God's grace enlightens our intellects, strengthens our will, orders our passions and weakens concupiscence. If you soberly contemplated the negative effects of sin outlined above, you were probably struck by the realization of how seriously we should consider sin. Now I want you to take time and consider how important Confession is as the God-given, healing remedy for all of these evil effects. The *Catechism of the Catholic Church* makes a compelling case for going to Confession even when you only are confessing venial sins:

> Without being strictly necessary, confession of everyday faults (venial sins) is nevertheless strongly recommended by the Church. Indeed the regular confession of our venial sins helps us form our conscience, fight against evil tendencies, let ourselves be healed by Christ, and progress in the life of the Spirit. By receiving more frequently through this sacrament the gift of the Father's mercy, we are spurred to be merciful as he is merciful. (1458)

One by one, let's consider what impact the regular confession of our venial sins will have on our lives:

1. *My conscience will be formed.* What's our conscience? It's the secret sanctuary in the depth of our hearts where we encounter God and hear His voice. It's that "voice" that emerges from deep within us that is not our own voice (even if we hear it as our own voice) that prompts us to do or to avoid some thought, word or deed. We feel or sense God's presence, and what is in accord with God and what is not. Pope Paul VI called these our "religious sense" and our "sense of sin." Pope John Paul II, in his Apostolic Exhortation, On Reconciliation and Penance, wrote about the inseparable link between the vitality and profundity of our sense of God and our sense of sin:

> This sense [of sin] is rooted in man's moral conscience and is as it were its thermometer. It is linked to the sense of God, since it derives from man's conscious relationship with God as his Creator, Lord and Father...When the conscience is weakened the sense of God is also obscured, and as a result, with the loss of this decisive inner point of reference, the sense of sin is lost.[2]

2. John Paul II, Apostolic Exhortation on Penance and Reconciliation *Reconciliatio et Paenitentia* (December 2, 1984), §17 at www.nccbuscc.org/pope/writings.htm

As Confession forms our conscience it revives our sense of God and our sense of sin. Without a vital sense of God, we lose the "decisive inner point of reference" for our lives. We fail to realize that we belong to God and were made for communion with God and we begin to live a lie. As our sense of God grows, our sense of what is sinful also grows. The regular practice of Confession should bear fruit in a stronger sense of God's presence and direction, and greater sensitivity to sinful inclinations, moments and temptations that touch our lives every day.

2. *I will gain strength in the fight against evil tendencies.* If this was the only benefit from going to Confession, I would be there! If you need help fighting against evil tendencies in your life, raise your hand. Ask me and I'll raise both hands high, like a guilty man who was just caught and surrenders, or like a small boy asking to be picked up by his father. Confession is all of that and more; it's a moment of surrendering as a guilty man, but surrendering into the merciful arms of my heavenly Father. It's also a request for strength in my battle against the evil inclinations and desires that live in me. A regular Confession grants such strength.

3. *I will let myself be healed by Christ.* There's that word again: healing. Confession is all about meeting Jesus Christ, my Divine Healer. Notice the way the sentence reads. It doesn't say, "I ask to be healed by Christ." The sentence is structured in a way that emphasizes the initia-

tive and will of Jesus Christ. He wills to heal us. Am I willing to let Jesus Christ heal me of the damage caused by sin? He wants me healed. Jesus Christ can only heal those who open themselves to His healing touch. You don't have to guess or wonder what Jesus Christ has in store for you when you betray Him and end up destroying your own spiritual health. When you feel spiritually dead, go to Confession and meet the One, the only One who can lift you out of spiritual death and restore you. He's dying to heal you. Actually, He died to heal you. Please, let yourself be healed by Christ.

4. *I will progress in the life of the Holy Spirit.* This one line requires an entire book to unpack. Suffice it to say that your whole spiritual life is about growing in the life of the Holy Spirit. In order to live out the five sentences, "I did it. I am sorry. Forgive me. I will make up for it. I will never do it again," I need an intimate and profound relationship with the Holy Spirit. As we reflect on each of the five statements, we'll see how the Holy Spirit plays a vital part in empowering us to say and live each of the five sentences that will heal our lives. If we can say and mean these five sentences, that will be progress!

5. *I will be spurred to be merciful.* In my opinion, one of the most needed and most difficult challenges we face in life is showing mercy to those who have hurt us, especially to those who have hurt us very deeply. We want justice and maybe even vengeance. Showing favor to someone

who deserves the opposite doesn't quickly come to mind. Yet the capacity to extend forgiveness to others, to show them mercy, is precisely what will grow in us the more we go to Confession. How does this happen? It happens because a regular Confession brings us face-to-face with the God who has shown us continuous mercy and offered us nothing but forgiveness when we failed Him. How can I keep on going back to the Father of Mercies and asking for a fresh start and new beginning when I refuse to extend that same opportunity to others? The short answer is, I can't.

Some of you reading this may think that this section doesn't apply to you because of how badly you were hurt. Trust me, the Lord's desire to heal you extends all the way down to that place where you are spiritually sick with anger, resentment or a desire for revenge against those who have sinned against you. In the chapter on Reconciliation, we'll explore the theme of mercy and extending mercy toward others more fully.

These are some of the gifts and the graces that come to us when we go to Confession regularly. I will mention others in Chapter Five. If we avoid Confession unless we've committed a mortal sin, then we are robbing ourselves of the benefits God intended for us in the sacrament. We certainly need the sacrament of Confession in the event of mortal sin, but the graces of Confession were meant for us in our everyday struggles too, in those daily faults where we stumble and fall. Confession offers us something else that many people spend their whole lives searching for without success. What is that? Read on!

## THE DOOR TO PEACE

Location. Location. Location. Not only is that the correct answer to questions in real estate, but also in church architecture. Where something is located in a church speaks volumes. It was the location of one word, a Latin word only three letters long, engraved in wood, which had the biggest impact on me the first time I went into Holy Rosary Catholic Church in Tacoma, Washington. Not long after I moved to western Washington State with Kari about a dozen years ago, I saw the majestic brick church that is Holy Rosary. Built in 1920, it is an impressive sight for those traveling south on I-5, the interstate that runs through Tacoma. Since we didn't live too far away, Kari and I decided to go to Confession there one Saturday afternoon. I wanted to explore the inside of the church and see if I would be as awed by it as I was by the magnificent façade. But first things first: confess, then explore.

Kari and I knelt and prayed in a pew close to the confessional, preparing and waiting for our turn. As you might guess, in a church that old, the confessional was a traditional, carved wooden structure. The priest hearing Confessions sat in the middle. On his left and right were two doors for penitents to enter, kneel and confess when prompted by the priest. It was while I was kneeling in prayer that I noticed the three-letter word in Latin carved above the main door where the priest sat hearing Confessions. The word was PAX. Peace. That was it. Three letters were more than enough to get at the essence of what awaited those who entered the doors of the confessional. Peace.

There are lots of doors with words above them. Signs above doors let you know where the door leads (e.g. exit, enter) or what awaits you on the other side (e.g. the name of the store, restaurant or business you are entering). Where does the door to the confessional lead? To peace. What awaits you behind the closed door of the confessional? Again, that one word says it all: peace. Who wouldn't go through a door that they knew would lead them to peace? Who isn't seeking peace: lasting peace, true peace, peace that runs deeper than my present situation, peace that this world cannot touch or take away? People spend how much time and money on drugs (legal and illegal) and therapy looking for peace? Some people, including Catholics, are so desperate they would do almost anything for the kind of peace I just described.

GETTING IN THE DOOR

Then why aren't there lines for our confessionals? Because many people don't know how to translate PAX from a word in Latin *above* the confessional to what happens *in* the confessional. PAX gets lost in translation. I know it did for me, growing up Catholic. Peace was the last thing I felt as I waited outside the confessional; *anxiety* was closer to the truth. Upon exiting? *Relief* was probably the word that best described what I most commonly experienced when I was leaving the confessional. Relief is not the same as peace. God intends you and me to experience peace when we go to Confession. The Prince of Peace, Jesus Christ, awaits us in the confessional. He is at work in the priest-confessor in order to grant the merciful forgiveness that has peace as its most beautiful fruit. That's what awaits us, but we have to go through the door. That's where the challenge lies.

Thankfully, we don't face this challenge alone. Jesus is with us. He is able to get through any door, even locked doors with the sign "Keep Out" on them. The Gospel of John recounts how, on the first Easter Sunday evening, Jesus appeared to His apostles while they were in the Upper Room, even though the door was locked because of their fear. His first words to them? "Peace be with you." He showed them His pierced hands and side, and the disciples rejoiced. He said again, "Peace be with you." He then sent His apostles out on a special mission: "'As the Father has sent me, so I send you.' And when he had said this, he breathed on them and said to them, 'Receive the holy Spirit. Whose sins you forgive are forgiven them, and whose sins you retain are retained'" (John 20: 19–21). This

Scripture account has themes connected with Confession all through it. Like the apostles, there are times in our lives when we are tempted to close and lock the door to our hearts and hide from God out of shame and guilt. It is in Confession where we allow the Risen Lord Jesus to show up behind those locked doors and speak to us those same words, "Peace be with you."

## WALKING THE PATH TO PEACE

Notice that I said it was Jesus Christ Who would speak those words to you TODAY in Confession. How can that be? In the Scripture passage above, Jesus not only speaks to His apostles, He also breathes on them the gift of His Holy Spirit. This is a new impartation of the Spirit given for the sake of a new mission. He sends out His apostles to continue the work of forgiving sins, of reconciling God's children to Himself and of speaking those words, "Peace be with you."

Behind that closed door of the confessional awaits one of those who has been sent personally by Jesus Christ. Yes, you read that correctly. Two thousand years later the sending continues: the Father sent the Son Who sent the Apostles who chose successors who continued to choose successors down the course of two thousand years. Two millennia later, Jesus Christ is still at work in those He sent to minister His PAX, His "Peace be with you" to you and me. This PAX is so essential to Confession that it is even carved over the door! Believe it. Let me take that back, don't just believe it, experience it.

I know there are people reading this who haven't gone to Confession in a long time or who have not had the experience of encountering Jesus Christ at work in the ordained priest in Confession. You might be wondering what it takes to have that healing encounter with Jesus Christ in Confession, the one that bears fruit in peace. Of course, the first requirement is showing up. To "show up" doesn't just mean just showing up in the church or even in the confessional. It means being willing to do what is required to remove all that prevents me from receiving His healing grace in the sacrament, and the peace that will be its fruit. There are five sentences that express what is required of us: "I did it. I am sorry. Forgive me. I will make up for it. I will never do it again." Please remember that these sentences are not external impositions that the Lord holds over our heads just to humble us sufficiently before He grants us forgiveness. No, these sentences express the internal requirements that make space for His peace and that ready us to receive what He is prepared and waiting to give. If we want peace, we must be willing to walk the path that leads to peace. There are no shortcuts. So let's get started.

# PART II

# GET SET

---

# CHAPTER THREE

# CONFESSION: I DID IT

*Father, I have sinned against heaven,*
*And in your sight,*
*I am no more worthy*
*To be called your son.*

Luke 15:21

Before we were blessed with children, my wife Kari taught in schools, both public and Catholic, from the elementary school level up to high school. One story exemplifies an attitude she saw operating in every class-room wherever she worked. One day while teaching a lesson she noticed Bobby, a rambunctious student who sat in the back row, looking for chances to pester his class-mates. Every time she turned her back to write something on the board, she heard giggling and activity coming from Bobby's direction. Hoping to catch Bobby, she turned her back to the class as if to write on the board and then quickly turned back around, only to see Bobby throwing a wadded up piece of paper across the room. She called out, "Bobby!" He couldn't stop the motion of his arm, but still reacted instinctively with the words, "I didn't do it," as the ball of paper was leaving his hand. Despite the fact that he was caught in the very act of throwing the paper, the first response that came to him was "I didn't do it!" Denial. Self defense.

## EXPOSING OUR DISEASE

"I did it." Welcome to Confession! Doesn't it make sense that the first blockage to our receiving forgiveness is our unwillingness to confess that "I did it"? When we say "I did it" in Confession, we are engaging in self-accusation. Just as the word PAX is engraved over the priest's door in the confessional at Holy Rosary church, the words "I did it" could be written over our doors. The act of accusing ourselves is so essential to this sacrament that it is how most Catholics name the sacrament; we call it Confession. We don't talk about going to the Sacrament of Penance and Reconciliation, we say we are going to Confession. It is what we are there to do. Confess. State "I did it." In Confession, I bring my sins out into the open by accusing myself of all those thoughts, words, deeds and omissions that are contrary to God's will. I acknowledge my responsibility for rejecting God's grace and betraying His love, and seek to be brought back into right relationship with God and His Church. The *Catechism of the Catholic Church* makes this point beautifully:

> The confession (or disclosure) of sins, even from a simply human point of view, frees us and facilitates our reconciliation with others. Through such an admission man looks squarely at the sins he is guilty of, takes responsibility for them, and thereby opens himself again to God and to the communion of the Church in order to make a new future possible. (1455)

But I don't just accuse myself or disclose my sins before anyone. As I mentioned in the discussion of the sacraments in Chapter One, I accuse myself in that place established by Christ and continued by the Church where Jesus Christ promises to meet me—in this sacrament of healing. I accuse myself before God, and God's ordained minister sent to bring healing to the spiritual diseases that are my sins when I bring them out into the open. Here is where saying "I did it" is the first sentence that will heal my life. If I will not confess it, how can it be forgiven? How is the doctor going to treat me if I refuse to show him my disease? In Confession we engage in salutary self-disclosure. We have to show our illness in order to be cured.

Certain things grow in the dark, like mold and moss. When exposed to light, they wither and die. Sin is like that. When we expose our sin to the light of God's grace, sin will wither and die. St. Augustine said that Confession "lays bare the hidden disease by the hope of pardon." But we need to go further. What does it mean to say "I did it" in Confession? How do we accuse ourselves well? If you haven't been taught how to make a good Confession, you probably have lots of questions at this point, like "How much do I say? Are details necessary? Do I have to state the exact number of times I did something? What if I can't remember?" To answer these and other questions about accusing ourselves, I'm going to reflect on a passage in the *Summa Theologica* of St. Thomas Aquinas written more than 700 years ago.

## SIXTEEN ASPECTS OF SELF-ACCUSATION

St. Thomas Aquinas, drawing upon the teaching of the great saints and spiritual masters in our Catholic tradition, identifies sixteen characteristics of a good act of confession. He states that a good confession is simple, humble, pure, faithful, frequent, undisguised, discreet, voluntary, shamefaced, entire, secret, tearful, not delayed, courageous, accusing and ready to obey. That's a lot of traits! If we look at St. Thomas' comments about these attributes, we can gain valuable insights that will shape how we say "I did it" in Confession.

1. The act of confessing should be *discreet*. Discretion here means well ordered, whereby we give more weight

to more serious sins. When you think about what you are going to accuse yourself of in Confession, emphasize those things that are the weightiest matters. Sometimes, the temptation is to hide the most serious matter in the middle of a list of lesser sins, almost as if we are trying to sneak in the serious sin, hoping the confessor might miss or at least not focus on the weightiest matter. As difficult as it might feel, accusing myself discreetly means putting the emphasis on what is most grievous or serious. I will make sure that my most grievous misdeed is recognized. It doesn't necessarily mean that you confess it first, but it does mean ensuring that it won't be missed or lost in the litany of sins we confess. You might say, "What I am most sorry about is when I lied to my wife when she asked me what I was doing on the computer."

2. The act of confessing should be *voluntary*. Self-accusation is a virtue and it is associated with human excellence, though it rarely feels like that. In order for self-accusation to be virtuous, it must be freely chosen. If I accuse myself out of compulsion, it is not free and not freeing. In the final section of this chapter, I'm going to focus on how "I did it" is not only an essential part of Confession, but also of living a confessional life. When we make a habit of voluntarily accusing ourselves in appropriate situations in our daily lives, voluntarily accusing ourselves in Confession will happen promptly, easily and joyfully.

When that happens, saying "I did it" will have become a virtuous act. Until that happens, saying "I did it" in Confession will happen in a voluntary way to some degree, but it will probably happen only with resistance, difficulty and without joy. That's okay. As self-accusation takes root in our daily lives, we will gradually discover it happening more readily. It's like overcoming bad eating habits. For a month or so, voluntarily choosing to give up bad foods and eating healthier is an uphill battle. You resist it, but eventually new, healthier eating habits form and you will give up unhealthy foods easily, quickly and joyfully.

The alternative is not attractive. If you refuse to voluntarily address those bad eating habits, a day will probably come when you no longer have a choice. An emergent health condition may force you to give up those bad foods or face more serious health ramifications, perhaps even death. What happens then? Most will stop eating bad foods, but do so kicking and screaming because it isn't voluntary, or it is voluntary only minimally. It is much more an imposition than a choice. Eventually you may come to freely choose what was imposed, but that is a hard path to walk. When you engage in self-accusation you have two choices: you can choose to do it voluntarily and eventually discover the joy that comes from self-accusation, or you can do it as an imposition required by Confession and suffer through it without joy. Those are the two paths. Make your choice.

3. *The act of confessing should be pure.* To be pure means it should have the right intention. It should tend toward the right goal. What's the goal? To be able to say the following: "I'm confessing here and now because I believe Jesus Christ intends me to do so. I honor Him as Lord by confessing. I confess this sin because I did do it. I am truly sorry that I did it. I want to ask God to forgive me. I want to make up for what I've done, and I will never do it again." There's a lot in those five sentences, but when we live those sentences our lives will be healed. The remainder of this book unpacks how that happens.

What's an alternative reason for confessing? Why else would we confess? There are less than pure intentions that sometimes are at work in our Confessions: "I'm confessing only in order to be forgiven. I'm confessing because I want peace. I'll do anything to get peace and if confessing will bring me peace, then I'll even do that. I'm confessing because I want to set a good example for my kids. I confess regularly because I want the priest and others to think I'm holy and see my devotion." If we are honest, we often have mixed motivations, if not those just mentioned, then others. We can experience a mixture of pure and less-than-pure intentions. When you become aware of less-than-pure intentions, repent of them, ask God to forgive you, and even confess them during your next Confession. That is the path to purifying your intention, to saying "I did it" with the right intention.

4. The act of confessing should be *courageous*. St. Thomas says that this means it should be an act that is immoveable. In other words, the truth about what I've done will not be denied or sloughed over when I confess, even though I am ashamed of what I have done and hesitate to accuse myself of it. The act of saying "I did it" involves facing the shame that makes us want to hide. But shame can also be salutary, meaning that it can help us find healing. How? When you are preparing for Confession, think of those thoughts, words, deeds and omissions in your life that make you feel ashamed. What you want to hide from your confessor is a pretty good indicator of what you should appropriately bring up in Confession. To do that, you will need courage to bring out into the open what you want to remain hidden. Courage will also help you find words that will accuse yourself in a way that truly brings out into the open what you did rather than *hiding your sin in the act of confessing it*, through vagueness. I will have more to say about this in a moment.

5. The act of confessing should be *shame-faced*. That seems obvious, but we often encounter the opposite in our lives. What do I mean? Have you ever been in a situation where someone is "confessing" a sinful deed but doing so in a boastful manner and even expressing pride in what is deplorable? When I was in high school and in college I would encounter guys who would confess their conquests or "how far they got" when they went out on a date with

some girl, or how drunk they got at a party on Friday night. They were confessing a shameful thing in a boastful way. Now that I'm older, I still hear it, often on sports radio stations or other advice-based, secular talk shows, only the sins have changed. (In some cases, not even that has changed!) Not many of you who read this book are going to boast about your sins in Confession, but what about outside Confession? Living a confessional life means eliminating all bragging about sinful activities, and it also means not showing signs of approval when others boast about their sins or commit sins in our presence. The *Catechism* has important insights to share on this point:

> Every word or attitude is forbidden which by *flattery, adulation, or complaisance* encourages and confirms another in malicious acts and perverse conduct. Adulation is a grave fault if it makes one an accomplice in another's vices or grave sins. Neither the desire to be of service nor friendship justifies duplicitous speech. Adulation is a venial sin when it only seeks to be agreeable, to avoid evil, to meet a need, or to obtain legitimate advantages. (CCC 2480)

Men, are you denigrating your wives or other women or letting other men get away with it in your hearing? Do you smile and nod when this happens even though you find it revolting? Women, do you happily tear down another person's reputation through gossip or detraction, or go along with it when your friend "shares" such talk with you? Whatever stage we're at in our lives, it's always a temptation to boast about something shameful, or to let others get away with it in the name of being agreeable. We don't want to cause conflict, or we want to avoid coming across as self-righteous by correcting or condemning such talk. What should we do? A moment's reflection reveals a number of good options. How about being silent? How about not laughing or expressing agreement? How about trying to change the topic of conversation, as if you hadn't even heard what your friend said? How about praying while this activity is going on? What about discreetly getting up and walking away without drawing attention to yourself? If this kind of talk is a pattern, then you may even approach your friend privately and share about *your struggle* to "only say the good things men need to hear, things that will really help them" (Eph. 4:29). Your confession of your challenge to face the sin of gossip or detraction may open her to see her own need to address this sin.

6. The act of confessing should be *tearful*. We should shed tears over what we have done. The idea of deploring the sin we've committed to the point that we would cry about it is an idea that can be a challenge for us today. What makes this more challenging is that many of us, especially men, are not accustomed to think of being tearful as

a goal; the opposite is more likely our goal. What will help us get at the essence of what St. Thomas means when he says that confessing should be tearful? The *Catechism of the Catholic Church* gives us the answer in paragraph 598 quoted below. Sin is a personal issue, not just a legal issue. Sin isn't simply about breaking a law (God's law); it's about breaking a heart. My sin pierces the Heart of Jesus Christ. If you recall pictures of the Sacred Heart of Jesus, His Heart is shown to us as crowned with thorns and pierced and dripping blood. Sin doesn't just gash our lives, it gashes into the Heart of Jesus. When I realize what *my* sin today does to Jesus, *that* can bring tears to the act of saying "I did it." That's when sin becomes personal. That's when looking at Jesus Christ crucified becomes a moment when I say, "I did that to You." The *Catechism* uses striking language to bring home the truth that my life today is connected to the sufferings that Jesus endured 2,000 years ago:

> In her Magisterial teaching of the faith and in the witness of her saints, the Church has never forgotten that "sinners were the authors and the ministers of all the sufferings that the divine Redeemer endured." Taking into account the fact that our sins affect Christ himself, the Church does not hesitate to impute to Christians the gravest responsibility for the torments inflicted upon

Jesus, a responsibility with which they have all too often burdened the Jews alone. (CCC 598)

What does it mean in the *Catechism* when it states that our sins affect Christ Himself? It means that God, who is beyond time, loads onto Jesus all the sins of everyone who ever will live, including the sins you commit tomorrow. What you choose to do tomorrow impacts what happened to Jesus in His Passion and death on the cross two thousand years ago. As mysterious as that is, it is also heartbreaking for us to think about. To borrow a popular idiom, "read it and weep." Or rather, read it, then meditate upon your decisions today in front of a crucifix and you just might begin to weep. "How I live today impacts what happened to you, Jesus. I did that to you. I am so sorry. Please forgive me. I will make up for it. I will never do it again." When sin becomes that personal, the five sentences that will heal your life come pouring out of you spontaneously and with conviction. As my sin comes to be seen in terms of its impact on Jesus' suffering, and less in terms of breaking a law imposed by the Lawgiver (the Lord God), my life will change. Realizing clearly and deeply that my sins today cause suffering to Jesus just might bring me to tears.

7. The act of confessing should be *humble*. For St. Thomas, humility is about "lowering oneself" before God, as a correct and authentic acknowledgement of my misery and weakness. This is the path to overcoming pride. Pride

is an attempt to lift myself up before God, and sometimes to stand before God in an adversarial posture. Pride views God as a threat to my independence. Saying "I did it" is a powerful means of humbling myself; it is a confession of my sinfulness and misery *(confessio peccati)*. Humility is a virtue. It is the opposite of pride; when I lower myself in humility, God lifts me up before Him in love. When I strive to lift myself up in self-righteousness, I am knocked down. In a later chapter, I offer further reflections on humility. For the moment, I leave you with a question to think about: are you drawn to people who are always lifting themselves up before you, or are you drawn to those who are open to acknowledging their limitations and need of help? The answer is obvious: the humble person wins friends and favor where the proud person repels people and is avoided.

8. The act of confessing should be *faithful*. St. Thomas means faithful in the sense that Confession must be a manifestation of our sinfulness, an act that brings what is hidden out into the open. If our self-accusation, our saying "I did it" is not true, we are not being faithful. On rare occasions this refers to people who go to Confession and accuse themselves of sins that they have not committed. Someone once told me he had done this out of embarrassment because he didn't know what to say. Don't do that! If you are in the midst of Confession, and don't know

what to say, just say that to the confessor. He will almost certainly be willing to help you.

The second, more common occurrence of not being faithful in confessing is when I have a nagging sense that I should confess something I'm thinking about and I am pretty sure that it is a sin, but I simply refuse to accuse myself. That is not to be treated lightly. Confession is that secret tribunal of mercy where Jesus Christ promises to meet you with His healing of your spiritual disease, but He can't treat the disease if you don't make it known. Not making a sin known in Confession is a betrayal of the sacrament itself; it is a sin.

It is more often the case that a person forgets what he intended to confess and then the moment for confessing passes. It happens like this: you prepare for Confession, go into the confessional and confess your sins. You say you are done and then the priest offers you some guidance or counsel. If you remember a sin you forgot to confess, please bring it up and confess it. But what if you remember while praying your Act of Contrition or afterwards? What do you do? Do you stop praying your Act of Contrition or interrupt the priest during his prayer of absolution? No, that is not required. Aren't you committing the sin of hiding something sinful that should be confessed? No, you are not. If you took the time and effort to prepare well for Confession and sincerely forgot what you intended to confess during your Confession, the Church says you are forgiven! Trust that the Lord's mercy covers all your sins, including that one. You are forgiven, but the Church does require you to confess it the next time you go to Confession. With that said, wouldn't it be better to avoid those situations altogether? I believe it would. If you prepare well for Confession, then this type of situation will occur rarely, if ever.

I recommend three practices for preparing well for Confession.* First, take the necessary time to make a good examination of conscience. Second, when you make your examination of conscience, write down the list of sins you will confess, and if needed, bring the list with you to Confession to help ensure you won't forget. You can refer to the list prior to going into the confessional and then put it in your pocket. But don't be concerned or embarrassed if you need to have your list in front of you. In time, once you begin going to Confession regularly, that won't be necessary. Third, at the end of your time of confessing, add a general statement like the following: "For these and all my other sins, those unknown to me or those I can't recall at this time, I am truly sorry and ask for mercy and forgiveness." That statement is not a way to avoid confessing a particular sin, but a way of being at peace that you've confessed all that you are aware of and can remember to confess. If after all this you later realize

---

* I discuss this theme more fully in Chapters Seven and Eight.

you forgot to confess something, trust that the Lord saw your efforts and intention to confess all that should be confessed. You are forgiven.

But even with those practices in place, imagine you sincerely forgot a sin that you should have confessed, and you are not at peace because of it. What should you do? Bring it up at your next Confession. Tell the priest the sin you forgot to confess, the fact that you prepared to confess it, but sincerely forgot it. Not only will you be absolved, but I'm confident the priest will offer his assurance that you should be at peace whenever this happens, trusting in the Lord's merciful forgiveness. The Lord and the Church do not want us to be scrupulous about our sins.

9. The act of confessing must be *open*, as in undisguised. How often when we go to Confession do we use vague words? How often do we dance around the sin we are there to confess? I am there to say "I did it" but end up saying in effect, "What I did specifically I don't want to tell you openly, so I'll disguise it by describing the sin in more general terms." For example, I have heard many priests say that it is common to hear men confess the sin of internet pornography. But it's easy to imagine that the sin ends up being confessed in ways that disguise rather than expose what happened, like the following: "I confess to going to some inappropriate websites. I confess to doing some bad things I'm not proud of on the internet. I confess to having conversations and seeing things on the internet

that don't honor my wife." These things are all true, but they disguise as much as they reveal. Self-accusation happens when we state in undisguised terms what we did. Someone confessing internet pornography might accuse himself in this way: "Several times a week, I spend as long as two hours on the internet on pornographic websites. I not only view inappropriate images and videos but also engage in impure conversations." That says what someone did in an open, undisguised way. There are other characteristics that develop and refine this point, which St. Thomas addresses in the next three characteristics.

10. The act of confessing should be *simple*. If we start using a multiplicity of words, we tend to make unclear or complex what was simple. In Confession we sometimes want to tell the whole story. St. Thomas proposes that self-accusation involves sharing only those matters that affect the gravity of the sin. How many times in Confession do you want to tell the story, and in doing so, reduce the gravity of the sin? "Father, I want to confess losing my temper, but you have to understand what she said first…" We want to give the context. Of course, this almost always makes us appear more like a victim of someone else's sin than the perpetrator of our own sins. Rationalization is another way to make complex what was simple. "I did it" becomes "I did it, but if you understand what I'm saying you'll see that I really didn't mean to do it or it wasn't really as bad as it sounds." In many cases, all that

is needed is for us to state in simple terms, "I did this" and leave out the context.

11. The act of confessing should be *entire*. This means that we don't suppress or hold back things that should be made known. This is the opposite tendency to the preceding one. In this instance, we simplify our self-accusation to the point that we say "I did it" in such basic terms that the full picture of what we mean was not made manifest. We should share enough details so that a clear picture of the nature of the sin is revealed. For instance, a man may not share enough information about an inappropriate relationship with a woman who is not his wife. In Confession, the priest may hear a man say, "I confess to having an improper relationship with a woman co-worker, but I haven't committed adultery," and then leave it at that. What is this man confessing? A flirtatious conversation(s)? Becoming too familiar or friendly (sharing personal stories or thoughts about intimate matters and cultivating experiences that create an inappropriate bonding)? Relating to a co-worker in a way that weakens her bond or esteem for her husband? Being playful and touchy in ways that don't honor his commitment to his wife? Being physical or romantic in ways that involve sexual activity without involving the marital act? You get the picture...now. The first self-accusation was so simple that it didn't make clear what the disease was; the latter questions give the entire picture and honor what

saying "I did it" actually means. These three aspects of confessing, that it be *open, simple* and *entire* work in concert to shape an appropriate self-disclosure.

12. The act of confessing should be *accusing*. This has to do with the fact that we are confessing to a man, but not just a man. We confess to the one ordained by the Church to continue the ministry of reconciliation in Confession. We should be accusing ourselves, and not defending ourselves, which is what we naturally want to do. I will treat the difference between the two in the section below on living a confessional life.

13. In the act of confessing we should be *ready to obey*. Our attitude in saying "I did it" should not be begrudging. What is involved in confessing well is the openness to hear what the confessor, the minister of the sacrament, has to say to us. Trust that the Lord is at work and will be at work in what the confessor shares with you. This is more important today than ever. I often hear Catholics say, "I don't know who to confess to." When I ask about going to their pastor, their response is sometimes a definite "No!" simply because of the prospect that the pastor will see who is confessing or recognize their voice. Or they may not want to go because they don't like what their pastor has to say when he preaches or offers counsel. Even if you don't agree with his counsel, use that as an opportunity for prayerful dialogue with the Lord. Ask the Lord to help you get clear about what you heard.

Remember that Adam and Eve hid following their sin of disobedience. By confessing, we are coming out into the open, no longer hiding. We are also showing we are ready to obey, no longer choosing disobedience.

14. The act of confessing should be *secret*. I will treat this in two ways, from the standpoint of the priest who hears your Confession and from the standpoint of the person confessing. Most Catholics are familiar with the idea of the "seal of Confession" which refers to the solemn, binding obligation on the priest not to reveal what was confessed. Here is what the *Catechism* says on this matter:

> Given the delicacy and greatness of this ministry and the respect due to persons, the Church declares that every priest who hears confessions is bound under very severe penalties to keep absolute secrecy regarding the sins that his penitents have confessed to him. He can make no use of knowledge that confession gives him about penitents' lives. This secret, which admits of no exceptions, is called the "sacramental seal," because what the penitent has made known to the priest remains "sealed" by the sacrament. (CCC 1467)

You can see how seriously the Catholic Church protects the "hidden tribunal" where we reveal what we see in the depths of our heart, in conscience. If we are going to feel safe being so transparent, we will need to know that our sharing will be held as a sacred act that must not be betrayed through being made known. Did you notice what else the quote above mentioned? It references the obligation placed upon the priest that goes far beyond not making known what you confessed. When you confess, a priest "can make no use of knowledge that confession gives him" about your life. This means he can't make decisions or influence decisions about you because of what he's learned in Confession.

Even with all these protections in place, some Catholics just don't feel comfortable confessing to a priest they know. If that's you, don't feel bad. For now, go to a priest that you feel safe confessing to. Go to a priest who doesn't know you. You may find eventually that going to a priest who knows you can increase the impact of Confession. Going to the same confessor over time allows him to become familiar with your spiritual journey. This helps him offer guidance and penances that are specifically suited to your situation in life. In Chapter Seven I tell the story of going to Confession to the same priest and confessing the same sin over and over. He was able to challenge me about that sin in my life precisely because I had confessed to him regularly. If I hadn't, or if I did but he didn't know who I was, he would not have been able to offer me the convicting counsel that set me free from the sin.

15. The act of confessing should be *frequent*. Aquinas says the well-being of Confession relies on Confession being frequent. What does this mean? It means that the full impact that God intends Confession to have in our lives will only occur if we access it regularly. How frequent is *frequent*?* On the one hand, this is a personal issue and there is not a correct answer for every person. On the other hand, recent popes have made strong statements about the power and importance of frequent Confession. Pope John Paul II, who went to Confession every week, stated, "Those who go to Confession frequently, and do so with the desire to make progress, know they have received in this sacrament...a precious light for the path of perfection."[1] Even stronger are the words of Pope Pius XII:

> For a constant and speedy advancement in the path of virtue, we highly recommend the pious practice of frequent confession, introduced by the church under the guidance of the Holy Spirit; for by this means we grow in a true knowledge of ourselves and in Christian humility, bad habits are uprooted, spiritual negligence and apathy

---

1. John Paul II. Address to participants of a course on the "internal forum" organized by the Tribunal of the Apostolic Penitentiary. Vatican City. (24 March 2004). www.catholicnewsagency.com/news/pope_says_frequent_confession_needed_to_achieve_holiness/

* This question is addressed in greater detail in Chapter Eight.

are prevented, the conscience is purified and the will strengthened, salutary spiritual direction is obtained, and grace is increased by the efficacy of the sacrament itself.[2]

Now that we have a clearer picture of what's at stake in Confession, I think as a general rule it is fair to say that by *regular Confession*, these popes were probably recommending a frequency of somewhere between weekly Confession and Confession every two months. Some readers may balk at this idea. Some can't imagine going to Confession every other month; maybe two or three times a year is more realistic. If you embrace the message of this book and strive to live a confessional life as expressed in the five sentences that will heal your life, "I did it. I am sorry. Forgive me. I will make up for it. I will never do it again," then going to Confession will become much more appreciated and sought out by you. What you do every day to live a confessional life will become an internal force that moves you towards Confession. Frequent Confession won't be a matter of conforming to an external discipline; rather it will be about allowing an internal impulse associated with being a disciple to come to external expression.

---

2. Pius XII, Encyclical on the Mystical Body of Christ *Mystici Corporis Christi* (29 June 1943) §88
www.vatican.va/holy_father/pius_xii/encyclicals/documents/
hf_p_xii_enc_29061943_mystici-corporis-christi_en.html

Confessing will be a fundamental vision for what your life is about. With my life I confess God's glory and my misery without God. What I do in Confession becomes what I do every day of my life. Life meets Confession. Life becomes confessional. You make room for Confession in your life. Regularly.

16. The act of confessing should *not be delayed*. One of the signs of our misery and weakness is the ease with which we fall back into the sin we just confessed. Have you ever had that happen? I just made a good Confession. I feel great. Coming out of the confessional, I have a strong resolve to "never do it again" and then two hours later I do it again! When this happens, one of the temptations I face, besides anger and discouragement, is to believe that I have to wallow in the shame and guilt of what I've done before I turn back to God or return to Confession. How can I ask God for forgiveness again so soon after having been forgiven? This is a trap and a lie. Do not believe it. When you've sinned, accuse yourself in all humility as quickly as possible. Do not let the devil take your delay to sow seeds of discouragement and even despair in your heart. Confess in your heart with contrition and do penance. (I'll treat what this means in the next two chapters.) Make a fresh resolve, and get the date of your next Confession on your calendar as soon as possible.

# LIVING A CONFESSIONAL LIFE: I DID IT

Living a confessional life is about connecting what we do in Confession with our daily lives. The first sentence "I did it" is associated with the essence of what we do in Confession; we accuse ourselves. The story about Bobby illustrates how unaccustomed we are to accusing ourselves in our daily lives and in society today. As I write this book Major League Baseball continues to struggle with the steroid scandal. Over the past several years, famous players accused of steroid use have come forward with bold statements of self-defense, denying ever using steroids despite the evidence. You did it. Admit it! I am not familiar with all the details of the scandal, but I can't recall even one player who stepped up and accused himself, saying "I did it. I am sorry. Forgive me. I will make up for it, and I will never do it again." At least one player came close to that standard. It was Andy Pettitte, a man who professes to be Christian. But even he nuanced his manner of self-accusation so that it sounded less like "I did it" and more like, "If I did anything wrong, I am sorry."

## COMING OUT OF HIDING

Our first reaction when it comes to sinning is to hide. We hide the sin or we hide ourselves. This strategy goes all the way back to Adam and Eve. What happened after Adam and Eve ate the forbidden fruit of the Tree of Knowledge of Good and Evil? Scripture says that God came to walk with them, to commune with them in the cool of the evening, and they were nowhere to be found. They were hiding. They were naked and ashamed. They were ashamed of what they had done. When they finally responded to God and God confronted them with the sin of eating the forbidden fruit, what did they do? They began to defend themselves, by pointing fingers and blaming someone else. Adam blamed Eve, and Eve blamed the serpent. No one wanted to take responsibility and say, "I did it."

Sometimes, when we are doing something sinful and enjoying it, we would rather remain in hiding and block out the voice of God speaking in conscience. That is never a good sign. When you are hiding a part of your life from those who are nearest to you, i.e. God (ignoring your conscience, the voice of God within you), your spouse or your parents or friends (through silence, telling only part of the story or fudging the details or by outright lying) and even yourself (through making the mental effort not to think about what you're doing or rationalizing your sinful behavior) you're in trouble. Living a confessional life is about living a transparent life. Confession is a God-given "safe place" for you to bring out into the open those parts of your life that you are tempted to keep hidden, or where you want to remain in hiding yourself out of shame or embarrassment. Learning to say "I did it" in Confession will help foster a willingness to accuse yourself in appropriate ways in your life. Transparency with accountability in a safe relationship is a great defense against sin. Defend yourself through transparency; defensiveness will decrease and humility will increase. Believe it or not, if you live transparently before others, in an appropriate and humble manner, you will find it freeing and a blessing. "My child conduct your affairs with humility, and you will be loved more than a giver of gifts" (Sir. 3:17).

CHAPTER FOUR

# CONTRITION: I AM SORRY

*There is a sacredness in tears.*
*They are not the mark of weakness,*
*but of power.*
*They speak more eloquently than ten*
*    thousand tongues.*
*They are the messengers of overwhelming*
*    grief,*
*of deep contrition,*
*and of unspeakable love.*

Washington Irving

With seven kids under the age of eleven, I can't remember the last time I got a full night's sleep. However, one night recently I came close. I admit I had some help from some pretty strong pain medication. A few days before, I woke up in the middle of the night balled up in pain. The pain got so bad I went to the Emergency Room, where they listened to my story and decided to do a CAT scan. They quickly discovered the reason for my pain; I had a five millimeter kidney stone that had left my kidney but had not yet passed. They gave me a shot for the pain, a prescription for some painkillers and sent me home. I wasn't thrilled at the prospect of taking painkillers, so I decided to try to make it without using the prescription medication. This was my first kidney stone and I naively thought that the worst was behind me. Was I wrong! Two nights later, I experienced how wrong I was. If you have never had a kidney stone, thank the Lord for His mercy. The pain was awful. I gave in and took a painkiller and within a short time was so drowsy I had to lie down in bed and almost immediately fell asleep. The medication did its job. It masked the pain and put me to sleep. A whole night's sleep!

When I was in the Emergency Room, the attending physician told me my kidney stone was right at the limit of what would ordinarily pass through my system on its own. Because of that, one treatment option was to wait for the kidney stone to pass all by itself, and to use the pain medication as necessary until that happened. There was no sure way to know how long the kidney stone would be lodged in my system. It would eventually pass, though probably not without some pain, and maybe a lot of pain. But I had a second choice. I could set up an appointment with a specialist who would deal with the kidney stone by using sound waves focused directly on the stone. Within a matter of several seconds, the stone would be pulverized into minute particles, which would exit my system without further complication.

That certainly sounded more effective and less painful than hoping the stone would pass out of my system on its own. However, I chose the first option, thinking that I'd just pretend the kidney stone was not there, mask the pain with the painkillers when necessary, and hope the stone exited sooner rather than later, with less pain rather than more. The down side to this option was that it didn't do anything to remedy the cause of the pain; it only masked the unfortunate effects of the kidney stone. And it dealt with the effect by making me much less effective! I couldn't drive while on the painkillers and I was basically useless until the effects of the medication wore off.

## A HARD HEART

This all too true story provides an entry point for reflecting on the second sentence that will heal your life: "I am sorry." When it comes to Confession and to living a confessional life, accusing myself by admitting "I did it" is critically important but not sufficient to receive all the healing grace God intends for me. "I did it" is the entry point, but I have a long way to go before I reach my goal. To go further, I must also be truly sorry for the sins I committed. The theological term for this is *contrition*.

When I say "I am sorry" I should be expressing contrition, or true sorrow. Why is this so important? There are several reasons that I will develop in this chapter, but the first reason is that contrition is the God-given remedy for what the Scriptures refer to as a "hardened heart."

What is a hardened heart or more simply, a hard heart? You probably recall reading or hearing it mentioned in key moments in the Old Testament: God sends Moses to lead His people, but they will not follow. God sends prophets to teach His people, but they refuse to listen. God chooses kings to ensure that His Law will be kept, but they give lip service to His law, and keep their hearts far from Him. In all these instances, God encounters in His people a hardened heart. They harden their hearts when they resist Him, by refusing to submit their wills to His will. What results from this? Nothing good! Ever! God punishes them for their hardness of heart.

I CAN'T HEAR YOU!

You may be asking what Scripture means by "heart," since it obviously does not refer to the physical heart in our bodies. The *Catechism* explains the Scriptural meaning of heart and the importance of what happens in the heart as follows:

> The heart is the dwelling-place where I am,
> where I live; according to the Semitic or Biblical

expression, the heart is the place "to which I with-draw." The heart is our hidden center, beyond the grasp of our reason and of others; only the Spirit of God can fathom the human heart and know it fully. The heart is the place of decision, deeper than our psychic drives. It is the place of truth, where we choose life or death. It is the place of encounter, because as image of God we live in rela-tion: it is the place of covenant. (CCC 2563)

There is much food for thought in this quote. The heart is that deepest center where I experience myself as an "I", a self, a person. We don't experience this center of our selves directly, but only by reflecting on our lived experi-ence. My heart is that place where I encounter myself as a spiritual and not just a physical being. It is there, in that place hidden from the eyes of the world, that I discern and decide what I will embrace as the goal of my life. My heart is a place where I encounter God and choose to live (or not!) in a covenant relationship with Him, which means a relationship involving mutual commitment, entrustment and obligation. When I harden my heart to God, I am refusing to respect the covenant or promise I made to be His faithful, adopted son. I am choosing to defend myself against His offer of assistance, guidance and strength. It's like when I was young and my mom or dad tried to teach or correct me. Sometimes I put my hands over my ears and said, "I can't hear you," or "I'm not listening." My efforts to prevent myself from hearing my parents, and the attitude it displayed, did not go over well. Yet, that's the attitude we take towards God every time we sin. Yes, you read that correctly.

## DOING IT MY WAY

When I sin, I am refusing to *yield* to God's Holy Spirit. Yield is a word we sometimes see when driving along a road that is about to converge with a second road. On the side of the road you will notice a YIELD sign. If there is a car on the other road, then you must yield to the other car which has the right of way. You merge in behind. When we agree to a covenant relationship with God, we agree to yield to the Holy Spirit. The Holy Spirit has the right of way in our lives. He goes first and we are to follow. Rather than "I did it my way," our motto as God's children should be "as the Spirit leads." The Holy Spirit dwells in our hearts. He lives in us and prompts us to think, say, do or avoid certain words, deeds and situations. We are called upon to yield to His gracious promptings in our lives. When I refuse to yield, I am choosing (with greater or lesser awareness) to resist God's loving guidance. I am willfully refusing to listen to God's truth speaking in my conscience. When I do this, I am choosing *I Did It My Way* as the theme song for my life.

Let me give you some examples of how this refusal to yield happens in little things and big things, maybe even daily, in our lives. The promptings of God's Spirit might stir in me the need to resist and reject a situation where I am tempted to sin. My heart hardens if I refuse to yield to the promptings and insist on playing with fire. There is no good ending in those situations, just a lot burnt fingers. I harden my heart when I ignore the nagging sense to go share my faith in Jesus with someone (maybe a friend or even a stranger), or refuse to reach out to someone who can help me come to know Jesus better; when I refuse to ask for or offer forgiveness; when I choose to entertain impure thoughts or images rather than reject them; when I give in to a temper outburst rather than control it; when I waste time watching television and ignore the gentle tug to spend time with the Lord in prayer; when I refuse to give of myself because it isn't convenient or easy; when I rationalize my non-involvement in a church activity or group despite the inner certitude that it would be a good thing to do; when I resist speaking uplifting, tender or affirming words to my spouse because it would be awkward or foreign coming from me; or when I tell myself ridiculous excuses in order to shout down and contradict the inner conviction that I need to give up a deplorable activity, habit or attitude. You get the picture.

## MASKING THE PAIN OF A HARDENED HEART

What we often don't realize is that the effects of our refusal to yield are cumulative. It's like a kidney stone.

Don't deal with it and it will get bigger and bigger until it is so big it gets lodged in our system. It won't exit on its own. One of the damaging effects of sin is that it fosters an even deeper attitude of refusal to yield to future promptings of the Holy Spirit. I harden my heart and it results in further hardening of my heart. Just as a kidney stone lodged in my body will likely bring excruciating pain until it is dealt with, a hardened heart that resists God and refuses to yield to His gracious promptings and inspirations will only grow bigger and harder, resulting in spiritual pain in the deepest recesses of my heart. I am referring to the emptiness, ache and restlessness that come from hardening our hearts to God. Like the kidney stone, our best option is to pulverize or crush our hardened hearts, so that resistance to the Spirit's promptings can pass from our spiritual lives.

But we have an alternative strategy for dealing with spiritual pain, just like I had a choice about how to deal with my kidney stone: painkillers. Rather than pulverizing our hardened hearts through contrition, we can try to mask the pain that comes into our lives when we resist God and refuse to yield to the promptings of His Holy Spirit in our hearts. How do we mask that deep pain? What are our modern day painkillers for hardness of heart? Millions of people are prescribed medication for anxiety and depression. Many of these people suffer from real physiological, neurological, genetic and/or psychological illnesses. Medication is an integral part of helping these people manage or overcome their pain. But I do wonder how many people use medication in an attempt to address the spiritual pain of a hardened heart that manifests itself as anxiety, depression or other symptom? Unfortunately, medication can never adequately deal with the spiritual ache in a heart that resists God.

Another way we mask the spiritual pain of a hardened heart may be surprising to many. What is it? Staying busy! If I keep myself going and going, involving myself in project after project, then I just might find fragments of meaning that give me at least a partial sense of purpose for my life. As long as that is happening, I will not have to deal with a larger sense of emptiness in my life. One other masking strategy is involving myself in intense experiences where I can lose myself: interactive video games, working out at the gym, gambling, drugs, drinking, a career, a romantic relationship or a dozen other alternatives. What is common to each of these is they have the capacity to draw more and more of my life into them. The experiences offered can be so intense and absorbing that I am able to mask but not fill the deeper emptiness in my life. These sensory experiences may be temporarily satisfying, but they are never fulfilling. Intensity is no replacement for depth. "Deep cries out to deep" (Ps. 42:7). The ocean of love in God's heart calls out to the bottomless chasm of our hearts. St. Augustine said it best, "Our hearts are restless until they rest in Thee (God)."

## CRUSHING OUR HARDENED HEARTS

Nothing in this world can cure or fill the human heart. St. Augustine defined the human heart as *capax dei*, as having the capacity to receive God. We were not only made *by* God, we were made *for* God. We were made for a relationship with God (CCC 2557). Nothing else satisfies; no one and no thing can fill the depths of the human heart. Close yourself to God and you will know a deep spiritual pain in your heart; it will ache for God. The good news is we have the alternative to masking our pain. We can crush the cause of that pain (i.e. a hardened heart), and receive a new heart, a yielding, receptive, open, docile heart. How do we that? Contrition. Saying, "I am sorry."

Contrition functions like the alternative remedy for my kidney stone. Saying "I am sorry" has the power to send focused sound waves that will beat against my hardened heart until the impact of those words crushes my hardened heart into minute particles. Because it has the power to crush a hardened heart, contrition is a profound spiritual act. *Being* contrite means much more than *saying* words that express contrition and much more than *feeling* sorry for our sins, even though it often involves an emotional component as well. A contrite person comes before God with a clear *awareness* of God's majesty and his miserable condition before God and without God, with an *attitude* of deep humility, as well as with *actions* (words and deeds) that express the "sorrow of [his] soul and [his] detestation for [his] sin" (CCC 1451).* How do I move from *saying* "I am sorry," to *being* sorry? Confession.

## CONTRITION AND THE SACRAMENT OF CONFESSION

Authentic contrition is based in an *awareness* of who God is, and who we are in the light of who God is. Seeing ourselves in a miserable spiritual condition of our own making is part of what makes us experience sorrow in our souls and detest our sins. We don't normally or naturally see ourselves like this. How can we be enlightened as to our true spiritual condition? The answer is that enlightenment is given to us as a gift by God. Without God's gift, we won't see our true condition, or at least we won't see it in its proper light. We may very well sense the spiritual pain in our hearts and realize that all is not good and right in our lives, but we won't have the full and proper perspective until we realize that *God shows us our condition by showing us His "condition."* When God reveals His majesty, I become aware of my misery, says St. Augustine.

---

* In Chapter Seven on the fifth sentence that will heal your life, "I will never do it again," I will show how contrition also comes to expression as "the resolution not to sin again" (CCC 1451).

When I catch even the slightest glimpse of God's infinite holiness and perfect fidelity, I become acutely aware of my sinfulness and infidelity. We see this in the Scriptures in several places. When the prophet Isaiah is drawn into the presence of God, what shows up simultaneously is God's holiness and Isaiah's misery:

> I saw the Lord seated on a high and lofty throne, with the train of his garment filling the temple. Seraphim were stationed above; each of them had six wings: with two they veiled their faces, with two they veiled their feet, and with two they hovered aloft. "Holy, holy, holy is the LORD of hosts!" they cried one to the other. "All the earth is filled with his glory!" At the sound of that cry, the frame of the door shook and the house was filled with smoke. Then I said, "Woe is me, I am doomed! For I am a man of unclean lips, living among a people of unclean lips; yet my eyes have seen the King, the LORD of hosts!" (Is. 6:1–5)

In Luke 5, Simon Peter encounters an astonishing display of the glory of God in a miraculous catch of fish. His reaction? To fall at the feet of the Lord and say, "Depart from me, Lord, for I am a sinful man" (Lk. 5:8). When John the Evangelist encounters the glorified Lord Jesus in the first chapter of the Book of Revelation, words almost fail John in his attempt to describe the holiness and majesty of Jesus Christ:

> Then I turned to see whose voice it was that spoke to me, and when I turned, I saw...one like a son of man, wearing an ankle-length robe, with a gold sash around his chest. The hair of his head was as white as white wool or as snow, and his eyes were like a fiery flame. His feet were like polished brass refined in a furnace, and his voice was like the sound of rushing water. In his right hand he held seven stars. A sharp two-edged sword came out of his mouth, and his face shone like the sun at its brightest. (Rev. 1:12–16)

What happens to John when he catches a glimpse of the holiness of the Lord Jesus? John tells us himself, "When I caught sight of him, I fell down at his feet as though dead." In this striking language we get an idea of how great a distance there is between God's majesty and our misery.

Now add to this the realization that God is my loving, patient Father, and I become painfully aware that I am His wayward son who has "sinned against heaven and against you; I no longer deserve to be called your son" (Lk. 15:21). The Prodigal Son is a parable that involves contrition, but contrition that is traced back to an enlightenment. The Prodigal Son, while in the pig sty is described as "coming to his senses" (Lk. 15:17). The Prodigal Son becomes aware of two realities simultaneously: he is in a pig sty of his own making, and he has a father who loves him and awaits his return. We need both realities alive in our awareness for our contrition to be powerful enough to generate an "I am sorry" able to crush our hardened hearts.

## ASK, SEEK AND KNOW

Enlightenment is a gift from God. It is a gift that God has in store for you and is ready to give you. But that doesn't mean you do nothing; you have a part to play. Your part is *to prepare yourself to receive His gift.* What does that mean? I'll explain by using an example. If someone wanted to give my family a piano as a gift, before we received it, we would prepare our home so we would be ready to welcome it. We would choose where we'd like it to go and then clear the space until it was large enough for the piano.

How do we "clear a space" for God's gifts and prepare ourselves to receive the gifts He intends for our lives? Jesus taught us—we have to ask, seek and knock for them. Don't get confused at this point. Our asking, seeking and knocking do not convince God to give us a gift. Rather, they do the work of preparing the space within us to receive what God originally intended to give. Our asking stretches our hearts until they are enlarged enough to receive. The *Catechism* quotes St. Augustine on this point: "God wills that our desire should be exercised in prayer, that we may be able to receive what he is prepared to give." (CCC 2737)

You can be confident that our asking, seeking and knocking in prayer will be answered. Why? Because God wants to reveal Himself to you and reveal your condition to yourself more than you want it. God is with you right now, nearer to you than you can possibly imagine. He is waiting on your prayer, on your opening your heart to Him. Begin right now; ask, seek and knock every day, several times a day, for God to show you His majesty, holiness, fidelity and fatherliness, and in the light of His glory you will also come to see your misery. Call out to Him, "I want to see You. Show me Your face." That is our heavenly destiny, to see God. Pray that it begins here and now in your life, to the degree that this is possible. He will answer your prayer, not because you deserve it, but because He delights in you.

Your awareness of God's majesty and your misery will probably grow gradually, but maybe not. You may be drawn into an encounter with Jesus Christ like that of John the Evangelist, the writer of the Book of Revelation. If it doesn't happen immediately, how will you know that such an enlightenment is happening at all? What effect does this enlightenment have on your life? Pope John Paul II wrote that when a truth comes alive in our *awareness* it gives birth to a new *attitude* or *way of relating* to something or someone. When God reveals His majesty and our misery, the new attitude that comes alive in us is humility. Humility is at the heart of contrition. Before we explore how humility is connected to contrition, I need to distinguish between what the *Catechism* calls *contrition* and *attrition*.

## SOURCES OF SORROW AND FEAR

Growing up, I loved playing Little League baseball. My favorite games were when I got to pitch. To be more precise, my favorite games were the games when I pitched well! I remember one game I was pitching that I would not classify as a favorite. I had given up a few runs during the game and was in a jam trying to get out of another inning. The bases were full and I knew I couldn't afford to give up another run. I remember looking over at my teammates in the dugout, and then noticing the coach. He was looking at me intently with a serious look on his face. He was not happy. It was abundantly clear to me if I didn't get this next batter out, I was going to be taken out of the game. There was no doubt in my mind. I knew what was at stake. I started sweating. I knew I had better produce or else!

But then I looked up over the dugout at the crowd watching the game from the bleachers, and I saw my dad, who was also looking right at me. What was so striking was the difference in what I saw in his eyes and in the smile on his face. I saw love in his eyes, and support and encouragement in his smile. That impacted me so differently than the look on the face of the coach. I wanted to get this next batter out, not because I was afraid of being pulled out of the game, but because I wanted to make my dad proud! I loved my dad. He was watching me. I didn't want to let him down. What a different impact my dad's presence had on me compared to knowing that my coach was watching and waiting to take me out of the game if I didn't do well.

On the pitcher's mound that game, I experienced two types of fear, what Catholic theology calls "servile fear" and "filial fear." Servile fear is fear associated with punishment or fear of the negative consequences of my actions. I was experiencing a fear of punishment from my coach if I didn't perform well. When I looked over beyond the dugout to the stands and I saw my dad, I also felt fear, but it wasn't servile fear. It was a fear of letting my dad down. I wanted to do my very best for him out of my love for him. Our tradition calls that "filial fear." The *Catechism* teaches that sorrow for sin has two sources, *attrition* and *contrition*. Sorrow for sin that arises from servile fear is called attrition. Attrition is an imperfect sorrow because it's rooted in the fear of punishment. It differs from contrition because contrition is a sorrow for sins that is rooted

in love. It is a fear of letting down the one I love, my
heavenly Father.

## A SORROW ROOTED IN LOVE

When I say, "I am sorry" in Confession, it is to be
first and foremost an expression of contrition. We are
called to a sorrow for our sins that is rooted in love. Even
though attrition or fear of punishment is also at work, we
should not settle for attrition as our primary motivation
for confessing. We often begin with attrition, at least I did,
especially when I was growing up. Don't get me wrong,
when it comes to sorrow for our sins, we should have a fear
of the consequences. We should be sorry for the punishment that will come to our lives as a result of sinning. But
that will rarely be a sufficient, long-term defense against
sin. Why? Attrition does not crush the hardened heart,
only contrition does, according to St. Thomas Aquinas.
In addition, St. Thomas teaches that attrition will never
become contrition. Sorrow rooted in a fear of punishment
will not eventually lead to sorrow rooted in love. Many
of us associate going to Confession with the experience
of servile fear. If that is our only motivation, our hardened hearts will not be crushed. Confession involves both
sorrow rooted in punishment and sorrow rooted in love.

Do you remember the *Act of Contrition* you were
taught growing up? The version I memorized expresses

both attrition and contrition, with the emphasis being on contrition:

Oh my God I am heartily sorry,
for having offended thee,
and I detest all of my sins because I dread the loss
of heaven
and the pains of hell,
but most of all, because they have offended
You my God,
Who art all-good and is deserving of all my love.
I firmly resolve
with the help of thy grace,
to confess my sins,
do penance and amend my life.
Amen.

According to the prayer, why do I detest my sins? *Because of the loss of heaven and the pains of hell.* That's sorrow based in servile fear or fear of the consequences—attrition. *But most of all, because they have offended You my God, who art all-good and deserving of all my love.* That is a statement of sorrow based on filial fear or fear rooted in love—contrition. Even though attrition will never become contrition, the two types of sorrow, though distinct, are connected. How? St. Thomas Aquinas gives us the key: what links attrition and contrition is humility.

## DO YOU WANT TO BE EXALTED?

How is contrition linked to humility? Remember the definition of humility I mentioned when I examined the sixteen attributes of confessing in Chapter Three? Humility is lowering myself before God. St. Thomas uses the phrase "praiseworthy self-abasement" to define humility. He uses the adjective "praiseworthy" because humility is not just about putting myself down, which is a common misconception about humility. If all you do is put yourself down or "abase yourself," you will stay down. But if you lower yourself before God in a praise-worthy manner, He will lift you up! Jesus taught that the humble will be exalted. Remember, we only get the correct awareness of our condition when we see it in the light of God's condition. When I say "I am sorry" with humility, I am acknowledging the great distance that exists between God and me. I am saying, "I am sorry that I have not been faithful to You, as You have always been faithful to me. I am sorry that I have not honored You as Lord in my life." As we encounter the living God, we will truly know from the depths of our souls how great the distance is between His majesty and our misery and His fidelity and our infidelity. We are going see the truth and we will lower ourselves before Him.

## CLINGING TO MY OWN JUDGMENT

What I just wrote might sound easier than it actually is. Truth be told, we resist humility. In our fallen condition, we prefer the alternative: pride. Pride is the opposite of humility. As I wrote in Chapter Three, the proud person refuses to lower himself before God, but instead lifts himself up before God, in opposition to God. He resists yielding to the Holy Spirit. St. Thomas notes that pride is the beginning of sin. He writes in his *Summa Theologica* that one manifestation of pride is "clinging to my own judgment." So true! That phrase strikes too close to home in my life. How often do you say to someone, "You are right. I was completely off base in my thinking. I was wrong." If you are like me, the answer is probably either "never," "rarely" or "only when I'm forced to." I will admit it. Not only do I want to be right, but I am confident I'm right in what I think—arrogant may be a better word. I don't begin with the idea that I'm wrong and then look for someone to tell me what is right. No, my starting point is to think that I'm right. That's not so bad all by itself. The problem is when my starting point is also my ending point, when I not only believe that I have a sound judgment about something, but I'm unwilling to be moved beyond my position. Pride shows up as resistance rather than as openness to being led or taught. It's puffing myself up before others rather than humbly acknowledging the limits of my knowledge or judgment.

That's what St. Thomas means by "clinging to my own judgment." I know from my own experience that there is no easy way to get me to stop clinging to my position. Spiritual pride doesn't fear adversaries. Bring 'em on! Your efforts will only make my resistance more intense and complete. That's spiritual pride talking. Remember, you can't soften a kidney stone, it must be pulverized. What will help us foster contrition that will bear the fruit of humility? Something unexpected: salutary shame.

## EXPOSING THE DARK CORNERS

One of the aspects of going to Confession that holds some people back is that we feel ashamed. Shame is more than guilt. Guilt has to do with acknowledging or accepting that I am culpable or responsible for a misdeed. Shame is the embarrassment or horror or disgust I associate with the misdeed or with myself for doing what is shameful. Shame almost always has a negative connotation in our culture. There are several reasons for this; many forms of shame and shaming activities are harmful when we inflict them on others. We can also harbor an unhealthy sense of shame towards ourselves. This occurs when we see our misdeeds apart from the light of God's love and mercy. That's the key. God's loving kindness towards us is a light that shines on our lives. When His light shines into the dark corners of our lives, we will experience shame, but shame of a different kind. We will experience salutary shame, a kind of shame that is helpful to us, that draws us out of hiding and toward our Healer and His place of healing, Confession. Such is the shame connected with sorrow for our sins, with contrition.

The *Catechism* defines contrition not only as sorrow of soul but also as a detestation of sins committed. To detest something is to despise it vehemently, to be disgusted by it. When we realize that we have committed acts that are detestable and disgusting (and all sin is) then we will feel deeply ashamed. "I can't believe that I did that. I am so sorry." This feeling of shame emerges in the light of God's love. When I consider sin in a personal and relational way (rather than in a legalistic way) as I mentioned earlier in the book, sin is seen as the breaking of God's heart more than the breaking of God's law. As I have a vital awareness of how much I am loved and how faithfully God loves me, the sense of disgust over how I fail God when I sin grows in me. I am ashamed of myself for failing to live as a faithful son of such a loving Father. Salutary shame is rooted in our personal relationship with our Lord Jesus Christ. "I can't believe I did that," becomes "I can't believe I did that to You." Sin is personal. Shame, embarrassment, disgust over sin and detesting my sin all grow when I look at Christ crucified and say with all sincerity, "My sin did that to You. I did that to You. Any sin I commit tomorrow will impact what happened to You 2,000 years ago."

## LIFE-GIVING SORROW VS. OPPRESSIVE SORROW

Love shines a light on my sinful behavior that, in part, leaves me ashamed. The kind of shame that is connected with receiving but failing to respond to God's love can be a powerful means of detaching us from sin. The very sin that I thought I would enjoy so much, and maybe even found satisfying while sinning, is now, upon reflection and in the light of God's love shown to me on the Face of Jesus crucified, something that disgusts me. Contrition, and the salutary shame that accompanies it, has the power to reverse the experience I had when I sinned. Contrition crushes any pleasure I had taken in the sin and replaces it with disgust.

Sinning betrays the faithful love of Jesus Christ for us and it crucifies Him in return. In the Old Testament, the sins of God's People, especially the sin of worshipping false gods, were compared to adultery. Adultery is a good example for us to use in this context. A husband who cheats on his wife experiences lustful pleasures in the moment of his adulterous behavior. Later, when his adultery is discovered by his wife, the guilt and shame he experiences, if he loves his wife, will crush the memory of the pleasure he took in committing adultery. That's the power of salutary shame and contrition.

I am at a delicate point in the book when I discuss shame, sorrow and even disgust as having positive impacts on our spiritual lives and as life-giving expressions of contrition. I say this is a delicate point because there are many people who experience shame, sorrow and disgust in ways that bind them up, oppress them and consume them. Their experience is anything but liberating. It isn't their hardened hearts that are crushed; they themselves feel crushed, overwhelmed and trapped in their shame and self-hatred. St. Thomas Aquinas acknowledges this. He makes a clear distinction between sorrow that is *life-giving sorrow* (that is rooted in love and lifts you up to God) and *oppressive sorrow* (that is rooted in an attitude of hopelessness and weighs you down). St. Thomas says that life-giving sorrow is accompanied by joy. It is like the Prodigal Son at the moment he is embraced by his father. Is he sorrowful or joyful? The answer is yes! He is both. Sorrowful at what he has done to his father and himself, and overwhelmed by joy at the love of his father who celebrates his return home. If you are sorrowful, ashamed and disgusted with what you have done and with yourself, ask yourself if those sentiments lead you to your heavenly Father (like the Prodigal Son) or are they all-consuming and make you conclude that there is no hope for one as hateful as yourself? The first experience of shame arises from an encounter with the love of God, the second can have many sources, but none of them lift us up or are accompanied by joy. One of these sources is sin.

Sin, choosing to turn from God, can result in our resisting God and closing ourselves off from Him and His love. It can leave us in a situation of disgust, sorrow and shame that deadens us spiritually. The more we are loved by God and love God, the more sorrowful we are that we have sinned. But the shame, sorrow and disgust we feel are not separate from the light of God's love that shines on us and beckons us home. That love of God reaches out to us each day, and each day we are called to live a confessional life, a life where we confess our faith, by confessing God's glory and our misery. A life that confesses God's love will give rise to a sorrow that heals, frees and brings joy. That is what God wills for us. The alternative? Experiencing our misery without knowing God's love and experiencing self-hatred, disgust and shame in a sorrow that hurts, oppresses and consumes us. I don't wish that on anyone. Neither does God.

## LIVING A CONFESSIONAL LIFE

Although I am not a priest, I did spend five years in the seminary discerning that vocation. For three of those years I lived with other seminarians from the United States and Canada studying for the diocesan priesthood at the Pontifical North American College in Rome. When you walk in the front door of the North American College, there on the floor of the foyer, inlaid in stone, is the coat of arms and the motto of the college. The motto, *Firmum est cor meum,* is taken from Psalm 107 and it means "Steadfast is my heart." My heart is true to the Lord. I am faithful. What a beautiful and challenging motto to live out, especially for those called to the incredible vocation of the priesthood. However, there was a joke among the seminarians, associated with the motto. It has to do with the first word of the motto, *firmum*. *Firmum* is a Latin word that means "steadfast," but it also can be translated as "hard." Translated like that, the motto takes on a very different meaning, "Hard is my heart." It was always good for a laugh when I would give a tour of the seminary to friends or others visiting from the United States. Is the motto of the school "Steadfast is my heart" or "Hard is my heart"? Ironically, it's not only humorous that the motto can be translated in two ways—it also speaks a powerful truth about our daily lives as disciples.

Today in your relationship with the Lord, and in mine, there is one statement that will certainly be true: *firmum est cor meum*. The question is, how will my life today translate that motto? If I am saying "steadfast is my heart" I am saying that my heart is faithful, yielding and ready to be led by the Lord. However, if I am saying "hard is my heart" then I am resisting, unyielding and unwilling to bend to the will of God, to God's purpose and plan for my life today. We can all take *firmum est cor meum* as the motto for our lives, because it will be true for all of us. The drama is in the translation. Some days we will rejoice that *steadfast was my heart* today. Other days, truth be told, *hard is my heart* will be the more apt translation of how we lived that day. The challenge for us is being quick to deal with those days when we are less than faithful. When I face a day that is most aptly translated, "Hard was my heart," the best thing I can do is to quickly confess the second sentence that will heal my life, "I am sorry."

"I am sorry" has the power to reverse the translation of my day from *hard is my heart* to *steadfast is my heart*. But only if I say "I am sorry" correctly. Saying "I am sorry" correctly is not a matter of translation, but a matter of intention. I can think of several ways people use the sentence "I am sorry" to express sorrow, but sorrow without contrition. Let's look at four ways of saying "I am sorry" that lack contrition.

## EXPRESSIONS OF SORROW THAT ARE NOT CONTRITION

1. The first expression of inauthentic sorrow is saying "I am sorry" because of the repercussions of not saying it. This is the person who says "I am sorry" in a calculated fashion. For example, saying it when it's the politically astute thing to do. "If that's what it takes to get people back on my side, then I'll say it." It's not based in authentic sorrow; it's a technique to ward off public censure or disapproval. Think of the apologies of celebrities or politicians caught in a scandal. They express contrition to salvage careers. They are afraid of the consequences or the fallout that will occur if they don't say it. Please don't think this

only applies to politicians, actors and sports stars. It is a temptation for us all. What motivates me to say "I am sorry"? It's a good question to ask ourselves.

2. At the other end of the spectrum from the calculated "I am sorry" is the spontaneous "I am sorry" that gets blurted out almost unconsciously when something suddenly goes wrong. Just the other day, my oldest daughter Mary Grace dropped and broke a water glass by accident, but not entirely innocently. (She knew she shouldn't have been as nonchalant and casual putting the glass away as she was, but her way of doing it was more fun.) When the glass shattered, her immediate response was a quick, high-pitched "I'm sorry. I'm sorry." That wasn't the first or the last time a scenario like that will play itself out in our home. We've all done it. The point is that "Sorry. Sorry." can become the immediate, default response that says in effect, "I can't believe that happened. I didn't want or intend that to happen, and I know I am probably in trouble because it happened. Please don't punish me...or punish me too severely." This use of "I am sorry" only rises to the level of attrition, of that sorrow that is rooted in the fear of punishment. We are called to contrition, to the fear that is rooted in love.

3. Most adults are not that likely to fall into the first two uses of "I am sorry." We are likely to at least be tempted by the third. It's when we say "I am sorry" but actually mean (and maybe even say), "I'm sorry you were

offended," or "I'm sorry that you were hurt." Here, the sorrow is deflected away from me (and what I did) and is focused on you and how you are relating to my action. There is no self-accusation here, no "I did it" as part of the equation. If you find yourself saying "I am sorry" like this, please know that it is not often well received. It can even be offensive. If you hurt me through your sinful actions, I am first of all not interested in your supposed sympathy for my hurt feelings. I am very much interested in hearing the self-accusation that stands behind your sorrow. In fact, when you state plainly that "I did it. I am sorry," you are likely to win lots of favor and sympathy from me. People are often more merciful than we give them credit for. Unless of course, we choose to use "I did it. I am sorry," as a technique to win sympathy. When we do that, we've fallen back into the first wrong use of "I am sorry" listed above. "I am sorry" must never be a technique used to win favor, but an authentic expression of what is within me.

4. Somewhat akin to the previous use of "I am sorry" is when we express sorrow for *what happened* rather than for *what I did*. This is an example of a bad effect that lacks a bad cause; the responsible agent of the action (that's me!) has disappeared. When I say, "I'm sorry that happened," or "I feel bad about that," I take no ownership for the action or the deed; I hide it in the passive voice (that happened) rather than accusing myself in the active voice (I did that).

What is common in all of these failures to say simply and cleanly "I am sorry" is a lack of humility to accuse myself by saying "I did it," and a lack of love which realizes that I've hurt someone I should love.

## KNOW THYSELF

Learning how to say "I am sorry" is one thing. Recognizing and accepting how contrition will live in you and be expressed by you is also important. There is no one universal way of expressing contrition that you should try to imitate. Rather, follow Socrates' favorite axiom, "Know thyself." Try to be aware of the ways that sorrow for your sins lives in you and comes to expression in your life. Some of us have temperaments that are more naturally sensitized towards our deeply felt inner states, including feelings of contrition. Some of us were born in or live in a culture where expressing sorrow (among other feelings) in words and emotions is accepted and expected. Others are more naturally reserved, or come from cultures or traditions where feelings are not openly displayed. Choose a manifestation of sensible sorrow that suits you, bearing in mind that how you express sensible sorrow will be associated with your personal history, culture and temperament. Whether you fall to your knees, beat your breast and cry loudly with copious tears, or whether you sit more stoically and seriously from a visible standpoint but internally express your deep contrition, the critical point is being able to trace your external expression back to authentic sorrow of soul and detestation for your sins that is rooted in your love for God.

## FOUR WAYS TO GROW IN CONTRITION

How do we grow in contrition? I will end this chapter by outlining four ways to deepen the vitality and authenticity of our contrition that are recommended in our Catholic tradition: petition (prayer), contemplating Christ crucified, reading Scripture and acting contritely.

1. *Prayer:* This one is simple. In the end, contrition, because it is rooted in love for God, is a gift from God. It is an overflow of our being loved by God which is always God's gift to us. Ask for this gift. When you pray for the gift of contrition realize you are praying to know God's personal love for you more deeply. As you experience more profoundly God's love for you, His love will permeate all of your responses to Him, including your response when you have betrayed His love by your sin. Your response will be spiritual sorrow rooted in love. You will say "I am sorry" and mean it. You will be contrite, whether it is expressed with great feeling and fervor or more quietly and gently.

2. *Contemplate Christ Crucified:* St. Augustine has an important principle associated with contemplation, *I become what I contemplate.* I am transformed and molded by the primary object of my attention and concern. What

I gaze upon grows stronger in me. When you contemplate Jesus on the cross, you will begin to realize that He is on the cross "confessing" both the sins of the world (which is what I did) and God's love (which is what God did) on the cross. As this becomes more alive in my awareness, I begin to see what my sins today did to Jesus Christ 2,000 years ago. I did that to Him. He did that for me. It is a simultaneous display of God's glory and my sinfulness. Contrition is sorrow rooted in love. The cross is a confession rooted in love, in God's love for us. Gaze attentively and with devotion upon a crucifix and contrition will grow in you.

3. *Prayerfully read Scripture:* especially the Penitential Psalms or Psalms of Confession (Psalms 6, 32, 38, 51, 102, 130 and 143). These are Psalms that are prayers of a contrite soul who approaches God. The power of prayerfully reading these Scriptures is that they are the Word of God and not merely the words of men. Praying the Psalms is a way for God's Word to be sown into your heart. Pray one of these Psalms long enough and these seeds will take root and grow in you. You may not feel the sentiment of the Psalmists when you first pray these Psalms. Over time, these words sown in your heart will blossom and find a deep resonance and echo in your heart. You will grow in contrition as you pray the prayers of a contrite person in the Scriptures. The Word will become flesh in your life.

4. *Act as if you are contrite:* The path to growth in the moral virtues is through action. If you want to grow in courage but you don't feel courageous (and maybe are not particularly courageous) act as if you are courageous. As you act courageously, you begin to form in yourself the habit of courage. The virtue of courage comes alive in you as you choose to act according to it. Contrition is a moral virtue, but it is one that is rooted in a theological virtue, love, which is always a gift. However, that doesn't mean that the principle of "act your way into the virtue" has no application. Rather, as we take up the position of contrition, of expressing sorrow for our sins, we are disposing ourselves and readying ourselves to receive the gift of God's love that will give birth to true contrition in our lives. Don't get confused. What I am saying is simply this: if you don't feel sorrow for your sins, say "I am sorry" to God, and then say "I am sorry that I am not more deeply sorry for my sins." It is not a trick or a technique. It can be a heartfelt attempt to say to God how much more you want to love God in all you do, even in your act of saying you are sorry when you fail to honor Him. Doing this does not make God give you the gift of His love. Rather it fosters the readiness in you to receive His gift of contrition. This may seem artificial, even a little false. It might not be what you really feel. Speak it anyway with as much authenticity as you can. Repeat this often and it will eventually become real in your life.

We are called to live a confessional life, a life that confesses God's glory and our own misery without God. As we come before God in love, we will find ourselves saying "I did it" and "I'm sorry," but love presses on to the next sentence that will heal our lives: "Forgive me." To that sentence I now turn.

# CHAPTER FIVE

# PETITION: FORGIVE ME

*Were a soul like a decaying corpse*
*so that from a human standpoint,*
*there would be no [hope of] restoration*
*and everything would already be lost,*
*it is not so with God.*
*The miracle of Divine Mercy*
*restores that soul in full.*
*Oh, how miserable are those*
*who do not take advantage*
*of the miracle of God's mercy!*
*You will call out in vain,*
*but it will be too late.*

St. Maria Faustina Kowalska, *Diary* (1448)

I have been involved in church ministry work for more than twenty years. For a number of those years, I traveled extensively to speak at Catholic conferences, retreats and other types of church events. I did my best to keep tight limits on how long I would be away from home, especially after Kari and I were blessed with children. Whenever possible, I would choose flight times that got me home for my kids' bedtime. One strategy I used to get home sooner was to fly "stand-by," which involved me getting to the airport far enough in advance to get a seat on an earlier flight when one was available. My chances of this happening increased when a trip involved multiple connections and long layovers. I remember one such trip. I had finished speaking at a conference and made it to the airport in time to get an earlier flight to O'Hare Airport in Chicago where I would get a connecting flight home to Seattle. Once I got off the plane and into one of O'Hare's main terminals, I immediately went to the display listing departures, and discovered there was a flight to Seattle that was currently boarding! That was great news! I would get home hours earlier if I could get on that flight. I made a mad dash for the gate, weaving in and out of fellow travelers until I made it to the departure gate for the flight to Seattle. They were still loading! I went up to the counter, showed them my ticket for the later flight and asked if I could fly stand-by on the flight that was boarding. The young lady behind the counter was very accommodating and said that there were seats available and it looked like I would get one. I asked if I had time to make a phone call to let my wife know my new arrival time so she could pick me up earlier. This was before I had a cell phone, so I had to go to the nearby payphone. The woman said that would be fine and she would let me know when general boarding was completed.

I walked the 50 feet to the row of payphones and called Kari to tell her the good news. As we spoke about how things had gone at the conference, I noticed the last of the passengers entering the walkway to the plane, and a gate attendant closing the door to the ramp leading to the plane. I blurted out to Kari that I had to go, hung up the phone and ran for the door. By the time I got there, the door was closed. Despite my pleas the gate attendant informed me I was too late—they could not open the door once it was closed. Let's just say I was not a happy man. I huffed and puffed my way back to the payphone and called Kari again and angrily told her what happened.

Not even 30 seconds later, the young lady who had originally promised me a seat reappeared at the counter. I said to Kari, "There she is! I'm going to give her a piece of my mind." The last thing I heard before hanging up the phone was Kari saying, "No, Tom, don't..." to no avail. As I approached the woman at the counter she looked up, saw me, and then the light dawned and her eyes and mouth opened wide; she realized she had forgotten to get me on board. In a not too gentle tone, I said, "Remember me? You told me I would be able to get a seat on that plane..." Before I could get any further, the other woman gate attendant at the counter came to her defense, "No, she didn't. She said she would try to get you a seat," while the first attendant just looked on. That response only stirred me up more. I was livid and let them both know about it. Of course, this did not help me win any friends behind that counter.

When I was done, I went back to the payphone again and called Kari to fill her in on what I had said and done. Kari listened patiently and then said to me, "Tom, you need to repent for talking to them like that. You need to go ask those women for forgiveness." This wasn't quite the sympathetic response I was expecting to get from my wife, since I was going to all this effort to get back home to see her and the kids. I said, "No way!" Kari then gently said to me, "You will not be at peace if you don't reconcile with them. This is your chance. Don't walk away from it. Go tell them you're sorry and ask them to forgive you." I knew she was right. I didn't want to admit it, but truth was truth. "I'll pray for you," Kari said as we hung up.

One more time I made my way towards the counter and the two women who were finishing up their paper-work for the flight that had just departed. They looked up at the same time, saw me and froze in place; one nervous about what I'd say next and the other getting ready to argue again (or maybe call security). The first two words out of my mouth were, "Forgive me." I told them how sorry I was for losing my temper and talking to them the way I did; they didn't deserve it. The change in the two women was dramatic. They visibly relaxed and softened. I told them about my hopes to get home earlier to be with my family and how I got upset when it didn't happen. They were very understanding, expressed how much they appreciated my asking for forgiveness and told me about how challenging their jobs can be during final boarding. We were all smiles by the end of the conversation. Before I left I made sure to ask each of them, "Do you forgive me?" to which one responded, "I forgive you." The other said, "Me too. I forgive you." I turned around, and with peace in my heart, I walked away in search of my new departure gate. Kari was so right. I am grateful that she convinced me to do what I didn't want to do: say "I did it, I'm sorry" and "Forgive me."

## WILL YOU BLESS ME WHEN I'VE CURSED YOU?

As I've mentioned earlier, in this book I am reflecting on five sentences that are associated with what the *Catechism* calls the *Acts of the Penitent* in Confession. For me, each sentence is more difficult to say (and mean) than the one previous. For instance, it is difficult for me to accuse myself by saying "I did it," but harder still for me to be contrite and humble myself by saying "I am sorry." In this chapter we will discuss the third sentence, "Forgive me." In my experience, these two words are even more difficult to say than the first two sentences. Why?

Because the first two sentences are statements, the third sentence is a request. When I say the first two sentences sincerely, I have reached the goal of the sentences. Not so with the third sentence; because it is a request for something, I am not guaranteed a successful outcome until I discover whether my request is accepted or rejected. I can accuse myself by saying "I did it," and express contrition when I say "I am sorry." But asking for forgiveness, saying "Forgive me" brings someone else into the picture. I am not forgiven unless the offended person forgives me. I am vulnerable. I am *asking* for forgiveness. I can't compel or force someone to forgive me. It wouldn't be forgiveness. Asking someone for forgiveness puts me in a position of waiting, and not an easy kind of waiting; I am vulnerable. I may not have my request granted.

When I have hurt or offended Kari there are times that I still hesitate or stumble in my attempts to say, "Forgive me." Why? Because I am asking Kari to relate to me in a supremely positive way after I've related to her in a negative and maybe even despicable way. Contained in the request for forgiveness is the realization that even though I did "curse" her, I am asking her to "bless" me. Even though I hurt you, I am asking you to help me. Who is naturally inclined to do that? Not me. So, we resist doing it. We would rather it be enough to say, "I did it" and "I am sorry." Isn't that sufficient? It is not. We need to acknowledge that when we do things that hurt others, we have to ask for forgiveness for what we've done, and for the damage we've caused to them, to our relationship and to ourselves. That's a tall order. How do we get there? What will move us to say "Forgive me" under those conditions? The answer is found in one word: mercy.

## THE SACRAMENT OF RECONCILIATION

To this point in the book, I've been referring to what the *Catechism* calls the Sacrament of Penance and Reconciliation as Confession. Calling the sacrament Confession puts the emphasis on what *we do* (we confess our sins) and also connects Confession to the traditional idea that our whole lives as disciples are to be a *confession of faith (confessio fidei)*, a testimony or witness to both *God's glory (confessio gloriae)* and *our sinfulness (confessio peccati)* and misery without God. In this section of the book, I am going to refer to Confession by another word, one which many priests and ministry professionals prefer when referring to this sacrament today. Rather than Confession, they call it Reconciliation. The *Catechism* accepts both ways of referring to this sacrament:

It is called the *sacrament of confession*, since the disclosure or confession of sins to a priest is an essential element of this sacrament...It is called the *sacrament of Reconciliation*, because it imparts to the sinner the love of God who reconciles: "Be reconciled to God."(CCC 1424)

Notice the difference in emphasis between the two. Naming this sacrament Reconciliation puts the emphasis on God's action, rather than ours. In Confession, *we* confess, but it is "*God* who reconciles." In this sacrament, our confessing is not an end in itself, but is a step along the path of reconciliation, of being brought back into right relationship with God. Jesus Christ meets us in this sacrament in order to forgive what we confess, but to forgive as part of His reconciling us with Himself and His Body, the Church. In this sacrament, the priest hears our confession, but he is there to extend what St. Paul calls Christ's "ministry of reconciliation" (2 Cor. 5:18).

Reconciliation is a word we hear in church but not often in daily life, even though it's something we desperately need. Reconciliation is about restoring union or unity between two people, parties or groups. Reconciliation repairs damage, heals what was broken, and reestablishes harmony and peace in a relationship. That's what happens in the Sacrament of Reconciliation—God reconciles me to Himself. He restores a union of love between Him and me by removing the blockage from the relationship: my sin. The work of restoration and healing is an effect of God's mercy.

Remember that the Church categorizes the Sacrament of Reconciliation as a sacrament of healing; it brings a spiritual healing to my soul by repairing my damaged or broken relationship with God. Jesus connects forgiveness with healing when He heals the paralytic and forgives his sins (Mk. 2:1–12). Just as the paralytic is made physically whole, he is also made spiritually whole through his encounter with Jesus and His merciful will to reconcile sinners to God. The healing effects of God's mercy encountered in Reconciliation are taught by the *Catechism of the Catholic Church:*

> "The whole power of the sacrament of Penance consists in restoring us to God's grace and joining us with him in an intimate friendship." Reconciliation with God is thus the purpose and effect of this sacrament. For those who receive the sacrament of Penance with contrite heart and religious disposition, reconciliation "is usually followed by peace and serenity of conscience with strong spiritual consolation." Indeed the sacrament of Reconciliation with God brings about a true "spiritual resurrection," restoration of the dignity and blessings of the life of the children of God, of which the most precious is friendship with God. (1468)

## THE EFFECTS OF RECONCILIATION

I wrote extensively in Chapter Two on the effects of sin. Here I will reflect in a similar manner on the effects of being reconciled to God in the Sacrament of Reconciliation. In Reconciliation, our encounter with Jesus Christ has tremendous, life-giving effects according to the *Catechism* text quoted above. Let's briefly examine each of these effects:

1. Reconciliation *restores us to God's grace:* I used the story of gashing my garden hose with the lawn mower as an analogy for the effect of sin on our lives. If sin gashes our spiritual lives in a way that weakens or cuts off the flow of the Holy Spirit, the "living water" in our lives, then Reconciliation repairs the gash and the Holy Spirit once again flows through our lives. What difference does that make? Read on!

2. Reconciliation *joins us with God in an intimate friendship:* The quote above refers to friendship with God as the most precious blessing that comes to our lives in Reconciliation. Jesus revealed to His disciples that He wanted to relate to them not as slaves but as friends:

> No one has greater love than this, to lay down one's life for one's friends. *You are my friends if you do what I command you.* I no longer call you slaves, because a slave does not know what his master is doing. I have called you friends, because

I have told you everything I have heard from my
Father. (Jn 15:13–15) *(emphasis mine)*

Notice that Jesus identifies us as His friends when we
do what He commands us to do. The reason we approach
the Sacrament of Reconciliation is because we have not
done what He has commanded us to do. Do you see
what sin does? It doesn't just break God's law; it betrays
our Divine Friend, Jesus Christ, and spurns His offer of
friendship. We sense our isolation from God through sin,
and we hide. Sin is personal. Jesus Christ established this
sacrament precisely so that He could bring us back into
friendship with Himself. He wants to be your friend. He
IS your friend, the best friend you will ever have. But do
we know this in our experience of faith? What is friendship with God like? Jesus gives us the answer. He says
about His friends, "I have told you everything I have
heard from my Father." Friendship bears fruit in communication, communication from God the Father through
His Son to you. As you develop your friendship with Jesus
Christ, you will see ever more clearly and deeply (knowing
in your heart) that God the Father enjoys you, He delights
in you. God smiles upon you because you are His. You are
known and loved to your deepest core. Your sense of the
Father's nearness will grow.

The best way I can say it is, God will become the *living*
God and no longer be merely a *concept* you believe exists
but have no contact with. For too long, too many of us

settle for saying we believe in God, but can't point to any place in our day-to-day lives where we can see God at work or sense God's presence. This will change. God will become increasingly real and alive for you. That is the fruit of our friendship with God. Losing that friendship with God is a devastating loss. Regaining it in the Sacrament of Reconciliation is more precious than gold.

3. Reconciliation brings *peace and serenity of conscience:* I wrote earlier about peace as what awaits us beyond the confessional door. Peace was defined by St. Augustine as *tranquilitas ordinis*—the tranquility or calmness that abides when things are in order and in harmony. That is what comes to our spiritual lives from participating in this sacrament. What is serenity of conscience? Serenity is the state of being clear, calm and undisturbed. Our conscience is that place in our hearts where we encounter God. Our consciences become clouded and disturbed through sin. We lose peace. Reconciliation restores peace and serenity of conscience. This keeps getting better and better! Why do we Catholics not go to Confession more? Probably because we had no idea that this is what God intends for us when we show up and ask for forgiveness. Now that you've read this, I hope you'll believe it, not because I said it or even because I witness to the truth of it. But believe it because this is what our Church teaches. Then act on it. But before you do, keep reading

because there are still more positive effects of going to Reconciliation.

4. Reconciliation brings a *strong spiritual consolation:* not only nearness, not only harmony and serenity, but consolation; you are comforted by God in Reconciliation. Your burden is lifted. You experience God's tenderness towards you. There is a famous painting by Rembrandt called *The Return of the Prodigal Son* which shows the Father embracing the returned Prodigal Son. That is an image of consolation. What we should not forget or fail to appreciate is that only Reconciliation will bring strong spiritual consolation when what ails us is sin. It is the forgiving Christ who meets us in Reconciliation like the Good Samaritan who pours a healing balm on our open wounds, after we have been beaten up and left on the side of the road by sin. Jesus Christ tenderly cares for us in order to restore us to Himself and to spiritual health.

5. Reconciliation brings *restoration of the dignity and blessings of the life of the children of God:* Confession is an encounter with the Father of Mercies through His Son, Jesus Christ that gives us a fresh start and a new beginning. We are like prodigal sons and daughters who come home to our waiting Father who puts a ring on our finger (a sign of authority and family membership), clothes us in the best robe (a sign of belonging to the family and a sign of noble status), cleanses us from the remnants of our pig sty existence and throws a feast at our return home.

Simply put, it feels great coming out of the confessional. As my 10-year-old daughter, Mary Grace exclaimed with a big smile after coming out of Confession recently, "My soul is totally clean. I can't wait to receive Communion tomorrow." A fresh start indeed.

6. Reconciliation brings about a *spiritual resurrection*: Remember the story of Lazarus in the Gospel of John, chapter 11? Lazarus died, was bound up in a burial cloth and put into a tomb that was then blocked with a stone. Jesus arrived four days later, commanded the stone to be rolled away and called Lazarus by name. Lazarus came out by the power of Jesus' command. The name Lazarus means "one whom God helps." In Reconciliation, we are each "Lazarus," one whom Jesus helps. By His authority at work in His priests, He commands the removing of the stone (our sins) that keep us in the tomb (of spiritual death) and calls us by name out of that tomb (restores our spiritual lives through a spiritual resurrection). Sin and its forgiveness involve the movement from death to life, from being stuck in the tomb to being set free. Let's reflect on this a moment.

## THE ULTIMATE, UNENDING CONSEQUENCE OF UNREPENTED SIN

I've already drawn attention to the effects of sin: venial sin *weakens* and mortal sin *kills* our spiritual life. We are spiritually dead, though we are still physically alive. Thanks be to God that He does not leave us in our spiritually dead condition, even though we deserve it. His will and plan are to resurrect the spiritually dead. For our part, we need to be willing to say "yes" to God's plan and go to that place where His resurrecting power is at work: in the Sacrament of Reconciliation. Hopefully, it is becoming increasing clear in your mind why we should flee from the "near occasion of sin" (i.e. situations or relationships that put us in danger of sinning) and fight with all our might against sinning. If not, then consider the ultimate effect of committing a mortal sin; it's an effect that impacts us beyond our life here on earth. What is ultimately at stake in mortal sin— when we betray God knowingly, willingly and in a serious matter—is missing out on the God-willed goal and destiny for our lives, that is, Heaven. To die *physically* while in a state of *spiritual* death is to completely thwart God's plan for our lives. You know what I'm referring to: Hell. Hell is that unending state of indescribable pain, horror and isolation of those who choose to definitively exclude themselves from God and His offer of Heaven.

Being spiritually dead while being *physically alive* is not a fixed condition. We remain spiritually dead because we choose to remain that way each day. In His goodness, God is constantly reaching out to us in mercy when we are spiritually dead in order to lead us home to Himself, to spiritually resurrect us. Sadly, some of us resist His loving address and remain turned away from Him. Our hardened hearts will either be crushed in contrition or they will harden further with every offer of mercy from God to turn us around. God desires our salvation. His "yes" to save us from our hardness of heart might encounter an ever-increasing "no" from us. We have to surrender to the pressure of grace beckoning us to repent, to turn from our sin and turn back to God. But this drama between God's offer and our acceptance or refusal does not last forever. It lasts only while we are alive. It ends with our death.

## WHAT WILL YOUR LIFE CONFESS?

What happens when we *die* in that state of spiritual death with our ongoing "no" to God? After we die, we come before God. Remember, we live confessional lives. They confess something! When we face Him at our judgment, our lives will ultimately confess one and only one word to the Lord—either "yes" or "no." If you are spiritually dead when you die physically, your life speaks a definitive "no" to God. His offer of Heaven is answered by our refusal. In the words of the *Catechism*, God permits our "definitive self-exclusion" (CCC 1033) from communion with Him. He cannot force Heaven upon us.

It is almost too much to bear; Hell is a real possibility for us. Not because God says "yes" to our condemnation, but because we refuse to say "yes" to God's merciful offer of salvation. Jesus asked, "What does it profit a man to gain the whole world and lose his soul?" Yet those are the stakes in our lives. As much as that thought is horrible to even consider, please think about it. One day your life on earth will end. That is for sure. After death you will be judged. You will come face-to-face with God. If we live a life that is hardened in sin, then we are "turned away" from God's Face—His infinitely holy, overwhelmingly majestic, immensely loving, merciful Face. Here on earth we experience God only dimly and obscurely, what will it be like when we face Him without the veil of the physical world? We will tremble in awe and wonder before this pure, perfect, eternal, all-powerful Spirit, *and* we will be almost irresistibly drawn towards the One Who is unimaginably beautiful and inconceivably merciful, personal and loving. All in the same moment. We will behold the One we were made for; the One we were made to love, to give ourselves to, to immerse ourselves in, the Blessed Trinity!

Ready or not, this meeting is coming. It is going to happen to you—maybe at a time that you see coming, maybe not. This is not a meeting to approach unprepared and in the wrong condition. If we are spiritually dead, with all that means, when this judgment happens, things will end badly, disastrously...words fail me. You do not want this. Neither does God. He wills Heaven for you, for me and for all people.

Wouldn't it be helpful if we could have some way to anticipate what will happen at our judgment, our face-to-face encounter with God after death? What if we could go to a place where we could experience something like our judgment here and now? We can. The *Catechism* uses this very language to describe what happens in the Sacrament of Reconciliation:

> In this sacrament, the sinner, placing himself before the merciful judgment of God, *anticipates* in a certain way *the judgment* to which he will be subjected at the end of his earthly life. For it is now, in this life, that we are offered the choice between life and death, and it is only by the road of conversion that we can enter the Kingdom, from which one is excluded by grave sin. In converting to Christ through penance and faith, the sinner passes from death to life and "does not come into judgment." (CCC 1470) *(emphasis in the original)*

By going to the Sacrament of Reconciliation when we are spiritually dead and saying, "I did it. I am sorry. Forgive me. I will make up for it. I will never do it again," we will experience the most important healing available on earth, *spiritual resurrection*. The Lord Jesus Christ meets us as a merciful judge and bringer of salvation. As we become more convinced through experience that He awaits us in Confession precisely to offer us His mercy, the less we will fear not only Confession, but also our Judgment after death. Why? The *Catechism* quote above tells us the answer: we have embraced a life of "converting to Christ through penance and faith" because we are living a confessional life, and thus do "not come into judgment."

The more you encounter the One who awaits you in Confession and the more you experience the benefits that flow from the Sacrament of Reconciliation, the more you will desire to go. What awaits us when we say "I did it, I am sorry," and "Forgive me," is an encounter with the mercy of God. That is the key. Once we encounter the mercy of God, we will find the most compelling of all reasons to run TO rather than FROM this great healing sacrament.

## MERCY SEES

I have referred to God's mercy several times in this chapter, but what is mercy? Mercy is one of those commonly heard words that is difficult to define. My favorite definition is the following: *mercy is showing favor to someone who deserves the opposite.* Think about that definition. It surprised me when I first heard it more than twenty years ago from a wise priest. For a long time I didn't have a clear understanding of God's mercy. My thinking about God's mercy went something like this: the Lord showed me mercy by forgiving my sins because He saw the circumstances of my sins, or He saw my good intentions. Mercy also meant He took into account the whole picture, all the good things I've done, and those good things clearly outweighed the sins I committed. More or less, I felt like I deserved forgiveness. Compared with so many other people, I was doing a pretty good job following Jesus Christ. What are a few relatively harmless sins when compared to all the good deeds I do for God, the Church and others? Surely, God will have mercy on me and forgive my sins. It was only right that I be forgiven.

## JUSTICE IS BLIND

Most people are surprised to learn that what I just described is not mercy. In fact, it's a lot closer to justice. Unlike justice, mercy sees the true circumstances, knows we don't deserve forgiveness, and forgives anyway. We live in a country where we strive for justice and for upholding a standard of justice in our laws. I am grateful for that. Justice is based on the idea that people should get what is their due, what they deserve. When someone breaks a law, he will be judged by the standard of justice. On the steps outside of the Supreme Court in Washington D. C. there is a statue of a woman seated, with her arm extended in front of her. This is Lady Justice, holding the Scales of Justice. Lady Justice announces to those who walk up the steps of the Supreme Court that under our system of laws, your deeds will be weighed in the scales of justice, and you will get what you deserve.

While this may be our hope for life in society (that I get what I deserve and so do you), our thinking needs to change radically when it comes to our spiritual lives and our relationship with God. You and I need to be convinced, convicted and firmly grounded in the truth that in our spiritual lives, we do not get what we deserve. In fact, Jesus got what we deserved. Jesus' Passion, His suffering and death on the cross and His descent into Hell are Jesus taking on Himself what we deserved. Jesus took upon Himself the punishment for my sins, for my failure to live faithfully in my relationship with the Lord. There is a passage in St. Paul's Second Letter to the Corinthians that expresses this powerfully:

> And all this is from God, who has reconciled us to himself through Christ and given us the ministry of reconciliation, namely, God was reconciling the world to himself in Christ, not counting their trespasses against them and entrusting to us the message of reconciliation. So we are ambassadors for Christ, as if God were appealing through us. We implore you on behalf of Christ, be reconciled to God. For our sake he made him to be sin who did not know sin, so that we might become the righteousness of God in him. (2 Cor. 5:18–21)

I mentioned Lady Justice was sitting with her arm extended in front of her, holding scales. I didn't mention what is on her eyes. She is blindfolded. What does that mean? Justice is blind. It's impartial. It's not personal.

Mercy, on the other hand, is not blind. Mercy sees. Jesus speaks from the cross, "Father, forgive them for they do not know what they are doing." He sees my sin. He knows what I deserve. Instead of allowing me to suffer the ultimate consequences of my actions, being separated from God forever in Hell, Jesus Christ, the Innocent One who "did not know sin" took onto Himself every sin along with every evil effect of every sin, all for the sake of giving us a way out of our hellish predicament. The Good News is that "God was reconciling the world to himself in Christ, not counting [our] trespasses against [us]." Our God is merciful. He sees what we deserve but offers us the opposite. He shows us favor when we deserve to be punished. Mercy sees. I am seen through. God does not weigh my good deeds on one scale and my sins on the other before deciding how to treat me. He is not blindfolded. He sees all of the ugliness that I heap upon this world and He offers me a way out. He shows me favor when I deserve the opposite. That's mercy.

## MERCY SUFFERS

Mercy not only sees. Mercy suffers. To say that God is merciful is to say that He does not remain distant from our sufferings. God suffers with us in Jesus Christ. Even more, Jesus takes all our suffering onto Himself, so that we never suffer alone. That's what the crucifix "confesses." In the last chapter, I proposed that Christ crucified confesses the sins of the world and the love of God.[1] God is com-passionate (from the Latin root which means "to suffer with"). He does not remain distant from our sufferings. One of my favorite Scripture passages from the New Testament demonstrates how close Jesus is to our sin and suffering. It gives an account of Jesus' encounter with a leper who asks to be healed. At the time of Jesus, leprosy was considered a punishment or a curse from God—a sign that you were outside God's favor. It was believed that the disease could be transmitted through touch, and since the condition couldn't be hidden, lepers were isolated from the community, and from their ability to worship God as part of the community. In the Gospel of Mark 1:40, a leper approaches Jesus:

> A leper approached Jesus with a request. Kneeling down as he addressed him he said, "If you will to do so, you can cure me." Moved with pity, Jesus stretched out his hand, touched him and said, "I do will it. Be cured." The leprosy left him then and there and he was cured. Jesus gave him a stern warning and sent him on his way. "Not a word to anyone now. Go off and show yourself

---

1. A traditional Catholic teaching that was a special theme in the writings of Adrienne von Speyr, a 20th century Catholic mystic and spiritual director to Hans Urs von Balthasar, one of the most influential Catholic theologians of the past century.

to the priest and offer for yourself what Moses prescribed. That should be proof for them." The man went off speaking freely about the matter, making the story public. As a result of this, it was no longer possible for Jesus to enter a town openly. He stayed in the desert places, yet people kept coming to him from all sides. (Mk 1:40–45)

Here is a man who is cut off from the community. He would starve if he didn't get help from those in town, so there was a set time and place where he could go pick up food. When he would come into town, he would carry a stick, rattling bells that would announce to everyone, "A leper is approaching. Stay clear of the area." He would get his food, leave the town and join the other lepers in the desert. A man in this condition, unable to hide his disease that was considered a manifestation of his being out of favor with God, approaches Jesus. He falls on his knees, a position of begging and a sign of his poverty and desperate need, and he cries out, "If you will to do so, you can cure me." How does this affect Jesus? The text states that Jesus was "moved with pity," but that doesn't capture the power of the one word in Greek that describes how Jesus sees this man. The word actually means "to be moved with compassion in the deepest core of his being." It is an attitude of receptivity to this person and his condition. Jesus opens Himself to the leper and welcomes him and his condition into His "innards" out of love for him.

That is the force that we should hear behind His response to the leper, "I do will it." It's an expression of urgent longing, of a deep desire. "I do will it. Be cured."

## THE TOUCH THAT COMMUNICATES HEALING

Notice what He does next. He reaches out and *touches* the leper. Jesus is not afraid of the man. He is not afraid of approaching him and touching him, of coming into contact with him, precisely at the leper's point of visible shame, precisely at the place in his life where he is "confessing" with his own body's leprous condition that he is out of favor with God. Jesus touches the untouchable. Remember what I said in Chapter One about the power of touch? It communicates. So also here in this Scripture account. Jesus touches the leper and the leper is cured, completely cleansed of his leprosy. He is now able to come back into communion with others. Jesus sends him back to the Temple. He can return to where God's presence dwells! He is reconciled with God and his community. He is not only made physically whole, he is made whole in every dimension. He is healed, spiritually, physically and relationally.

But what happens to Jesus? Jesus orders the leper sternly not to tell anybody, but he didn't listen and "went off speaking freely about the matter, making the story public. As a result of this, it was no longer possible for Jesus to enter a town openly. He stayed in the desert places." Just like a leper! Did you notice that? Who is the leper now? Jesus cures the man's leprosy by touching the leper. In doing so, He is portrayed as someone who has become a leper. Touch communicates—not only healing to the leper, but His touch works in the other direction. He takes the leprosy on himself. He makes this man whole, restores him to his community and to his relationship with God, and frees him from his physical ailment, not by dropping down some cure from Heaven, but by taking on the leper's curse. Jesus takes on the condition which brought isolation from others and from God.

## GO AND SHOW YOURSELF TO THE PRIEST

There may be parts of your life where you feel yourself cut off from others and from God, or where you feel ashamed about some past event or present situation, especially when you can't hide it. You may be tempted to consider yourself cursed or punished by God, and conclude that God does not want anything to do with you in your present condition. The incredible news of God's mercy is that Jesus Christ is not afraid of what you are ashamed of—not only is He not afraid, but He is willing to identify Himself with you in that place in your life. He is willing to touch you, to come into contact with you at that place where you want to hide, at that place that isolates you and cuts you off from others. Not just to be there with you, but to take it upon Himself so that you can be set free.

Not only will He do it, He's already done it! He did it 2,000 years ago, and He wants to bring it to bear in your life today. There is one place where Jesus Christ has promised to meet you with His mercy that heals: Confession. In Confession, what awaits you is an extended hand of blessing or even a laying-on of hands from the priest. See in this gesture a touch of the Lord Himself at work in His ordained minister of His mercy, the priest.

In our Catholic tradition, this story from the Gospel of Mark has been connected with Confession. How? When Jesus heals the leper, Jesus says to him, "Go off and show yourself to the priest." St. Thomas Aquinas points out that this sentence has been connected with what happens in Confession, where we "show ourselves to the priest" when we confess our sins. Mark 1:40–45 should be a Scripture that every Catholic connects with Confession. When I enter the confessional, I am meeting the Lord in my shameful condition that I cannot hide and that I desire to have healed. My confessing is my falling to my knees and begging the Lord Jesus, "You can heal me if you want to." The key to it all is knowing that the One who awaits us in Confession is so "moved with compassion to the deepest core of His being" out of love for you that He takes your sins upon Himself and communicates His healing mercy to you in the form of absolution from the priest. Jesus Christ not only suffers with you, He takes your sinful, shameful condition on Himself, freeing you from it, and identifying Himself with it on the cross. The crucifix is a "confession," a place of revelation and a display of God's desire in Christ to identify Himself with every condition, every situation that separates us from Him, so that we would be set free. His mercy is so compassionate that He willingly suffers with us, for us, on our behalf, for our sake and in our place.

If we were more convinced that what awaited us in Confession was a Mark 1:40–45 encounter with Jesus Christ, we would run to it! What awaits you is an encounter with mercy—the mercy that sees exactly what you've done, and wants to show you favor when you deserve the opposite. It is an encounter with the mercy that suffers for your sake and on your behalf so that you would no longer suffer from the consequences of your sins.

## LIVING A CONFESSIONAL LIFE

Receiving God's mercy in the Sacrament of Reconciliation does not end when we leave the confessional. It flows over into our lives, or at least it should. One of the most important fruits of receiving God's mercy in Confession is that we are led to be merciful towards those who have sinned against us. Paragraph 1458 of the *Catechism of the Catholic Church* says: "By receiving more frequently through this sacrament the gift of the Father's mercy we are spurred to be merciful as He is merciful." This is stunning because it is not natural; it is not what we are inclined to do! When someone lashes out at you in words, cuts you down, embarrasses you, or maligns your reputation, what is your first reaction? Do you say, "I forgive you. I offer mercy to you. I know that you deserve the opposite, but I will show you favor"? No! Our natural inclination looks a lot more like Lady Justice on the steps of the Supreme Court. We want justice! We want that person's deeds to be weighed in the scales of justice. We want the one who hurt us to pay the price for his misdeeds and suffer punishment.

That is such a far cry from how Jesus Christ treats us. Remember, He shows us favor when we deserve the opposite. He suffers in our place and on our behalf. His mercy does not discount justice; rather, it fulfills justice while going beyond it. How? By suffering the penalty for our injustices He got what we deserved. We love to *receive* mercy from God, but when it comes to *extending* mercy to others, that's another story. God freely gives us the gift of mercy, but we resist showing mercy to others. The *Catechism* offers us a sober and realistic assessment of our ability to be merciful without God, and then teaches us the path to being merciful toward those who have sinned against us: "It is not in our power not to feel or to forget an offense; but the heart that offers itself to the Holy Spirit turns injury into compassion and purifies the memory in transforming the hurt into intercession." (CCC 2843)

## WITH STRINGS ATTACHED!

When someone offends us, what happens inside us, deep inside our hearts? We become resentful, angry and maybe even develop hatred and a desire for revenge towards the person who perpetrated some evil against us. We feel justified in harboring these sentiments because we were victims, maybe repeatedly, and over an extended period of time. The idea that God asks, more than asks, even *requires* that we show mercy to any person who sins against us is incredibly difficult to imagine or accept. In this book, I have invited you to walk with me, step by step through five sentences connected with Confession that will bring healing to your life.

Earlier I mentioned that the progression through these sentences brings us face-to-face with sentences that are increasingly difficult to live out. We began by accusing ourselves, took a step forward to express contrition, then were challenged to ask for forgiveness. Each step was more difficult than the one previous. Now we face a requirement to show mercy! We learn that being granted the forgiveness we requested from God comes with strings attached. We who receive God's merciful forgiveness for our misdeeds must allow that mercy to take up residence in our lives and overflow into relationships and situations where we have been on the other side of the fence—where we have been the victims rather than the perpetrators. God expects us to be merciful to those who have sinned against us. It is so fundamental to our lives as disciples that Jesus makes this a petition that we pray in the perfect prayer He taught us, the *Our Father:* "Forgive us our trespasses as we forgive those who trespass against us." Did you ever really consider what we just asked God to do? We asked God to show us mercy only to the extent that we are willing to show mercy to others. How did that sneak by us? Was Jesus serious? Maybe it's a bad translation and we can find a different way of interpreting what He meant. Sorry, there is no way past this.

## CHRIST HEALS ALL WOUNDS

What are we going to do? How do we get beyond all of the ugliness that lives in us as a result of someone else hurting us with sinful behavior? Many of us try to get beyond our past hurts by burying them deep in the secret recesses of our hearts. We hope that by sealing up the hurts, we will forget about them and will be able to seal off the negative impact that they have on our lives. We might even tell ourselves that time heals all wounds. It doesn't. That's a lie. Jesus Christ heals all wounds. His mercy can even heal the wounds of other people's sins against us. We don't have the power on our own to deal with that darkness—all the anger, resentment, hatred and desire for revenge. We are powerless before it. In the words of the *Catechism,* "It is not in our power not to feel or to forget an offense." (CCC 2843) What a realistic perspective.

I remember a conversation I had years ago with a woman who suffered emotional, verbal and physical abuse in her marriage. Ultimately, she was betrayed by her husband, and then he left her. She was hurt on so many levels. I remember her telling me how angry she was at this man to whom she had committed her life. She was so bitter that he walked away scot-free from all the devastation and havoc he had caused. He was seemingly indifferent to all the destruction and injury he had inflicted. I agreed that what he had done to her was horrible and detestable, and that she didn't deserve it. It certainly wasn't what she desired, planned for or hoped for when she married him. But I begged her, "Please do not let his past actions continue to hurt you in the present! God does not want this for you. God wants you to be free from your past. He has a path to this freedom, but it isn't an easy one. It involves you forgiving your husband for what he did to you. You don't have to say it to his face, but say it to God and yourself in your heart. Ask God for the grace to forgive him even though he doesn't deserve it." She was stunned. "Never," was her one word answer. I pressed on, "Please, do it for yourself, so you can be freed from all of the bitterness, anger and resentment that continues to bind you up. Do you realize that in some way you continue to allow him to affect you negatively because of your unwillingness to forgive him?" She just couldn't do it. She didn't want him forgiven. She wanted him punished.

On her own strength, there was no way she could forgive this man. Please notice what I was not saying. I was not suggesting she reconcile with him, forgive him and allow him back into her life as if nothing had ever happened. There is a difference between forgiving him and reconciling with him—forgiveness is about showing favor where it is not deserved, reconciling is about restoring a broken relationship. In many circumstances, reconciliation will never happen, but that doesn't mean that forgiveness can't be offered, even if it is only in an interior, hidden manner.* In order to take this big step of offering forgiveness, she needed a power greater than her own. She needed the power of the Holy Spirit to set her free, to unbind her heart and disentangle her thinking, so that she would be receptive to God's mercy for her own life. Only then would she discover within herself a willingness to extend mercy to others, even her terrible former husband.

## THE HOLY SPIRIT WILL SET YOU FREE

Not only did she need the Holy Spirit to set her free, I need the Holy Spirit to set me free. You do too. Looking

---

* I'll explore this theme more fully in the next chapter on Satisfaction.

into our unforgiving hearts brings us face-to-face once again with our own misery before God. Too often, we are miserable failures when it comes to dealing with the effects of the sins of others on our lives. We are commanded to be merciful, to show favor to those who deserve the opposite, but it seems impossible. Now what? Thanks be to God the *Catechism* quote doesn't end with a confession of our misery, but an acknowledgement of our glorious God's desire to heal us: "the heart that offers itself to the Holy Spirit turns injury into compassion and purifies the memory in transforming the hurt into intercession." (CCC 2843)

When faced with our incapacity and helplessness, the Lord invites us to offer our hearts to the Holy Spirit. Entrust your heart, full of the hidden hurts, the pain, the anger, the memories and all the rest...give your heart over to God. What does that look like? It is a spiritual act that takes shape in prayer. The prayer might go something like this:

> Holy Spirit of God, help me. I am full of hateful thoughts, anger, resentment and even worse towards Jim. You know what he said and did to me. I don't know how to get beyond it. You want me to forgive him but I don't know how, and I don't really want to. I know I am supposed to be merciful but I don't know how to get there. I don't want mercy shown to him. Please, Holy Spirit,

take my heart with everything that is in it. I offer it to you now. I give you every moment I have ever spent with Jim, even those moments when I was a victim of his sinful behavior. Every memory, every image, every thought I have ever had I give over to you. Please, gently heal the wounds in my heart. Transform my heart, one thought and one memory at a time. Heal me of my sinful attitudes toward Jim. Take me by the hand and lead me through the process of healing that You have in store for me. Please, let Your mercy triumph in my heart. I need You. I am lost without You. I thank You in advance for all you will do to set me free; free to receive Your healing touch and free to extend your mercy to others, even to Jim. I don't know how You will do it, but I trust you. Amen.

## NOTHING IS IMPOSSIBLE WITH GOD

How will the Holy Spirit accomplish this supernatural work? The *Catechism* uses phrases that give us important clues. The Holy Spirit will turn "injury into compassion." The very acts which hurt us and left us angry will be transformed by the Holy Spirit into acts that evoke compassion from us. How is that possible? Remember what we learned about mercy in this chapter: mercy suffers. Jesus is compassionate. He is not distant from our suffering, but takes all our suffering on Himself. This is not only true regarding the suffering that comes as a result of sins we commit, but also regarding the suffering we undergo as a result of being the victims of others' sins. When you offer your heart to the Holy Spirit, He is able to mysteriously transfer all the sinful deeds and subsequent sufferings that hurt you from you to Jesus Christ. He in turn touches your life with freedom, peace and healing. When this happens, your life confesses the glory of God! Jesus Christ takes your place as the victim in all that you ever suffered. This mysterious, supernatural process requires much prayer. Some experience this freedom through silent prayer before the Blessed Sacrament, Jesus Christ's true and Real Presence in the Eucharist. Others experience it in deep contemplative prayer. Still others experience it when they are prayed with by believers who are trained to pray for the healing of memories. The Holy Spirit uses all of these means and others. He "purifies the memory in transforming the hurt into intercession." By His power the hurtful memories recede in our awareness. In their place come new images and memories of receiving the healing mercy of Jesus Christ in my life. As I grow in union with Jesus Christ in His suffering, my heart will be transformed by His Sacred Heart. Apart from my willing it or knowing how it happens, what will grow in me is compassion for my perpetrator, and even intercessory prayer. It sounds ridiculous but in truth it is miraculous. It seems impossible at the start, but by the end, we will proclaim, "Nothing is impossible with God!" (Lk. 1:37)

When God's mercy is not only received by us, but comes to be extended through us to those who have hurt us, we will discover the last fruit of mercy in our lives: mercy restores what we have lost. God's mercy not only heals, it restores. When we are freed from carrying years of hurts and decades of resentment, our personalities are freed to bloom and blossom in ways that we may not even realize we'd lost. "I forgot how much I enjoyed singing." "I haven't laughed so freely and fully in years!" "It has been such a long time since I was able to show affection like this." The sins of others shackle us. God's mercy not only forgives us our sins, but graces us to extend mercy to others...with the incredible blessing of being restored to the fullness of life, even the life we had forgotten because it had been buried under a pile of painful memories and hurts.

Extending to others the mercy we receive in Confession is one way that confessing leads to further action once we leave the confessional. In the next chapter, I examine what else is required of us once our Confession ends. I do this by explaining the fourth sentence that will heal your life, "I will make up for it."

CHAPTER SIX

# SATISFACTION: I WILL MAKE UP FOR IT

*Doing penance uproots the causes of sin.*

St. Thomas Aquinas

I have great memories playing as a boy in my back-yard with my brothers and our cousins (all nine boys and one girl) who lived next door. We had a large, flat backyard perfect for football, whiffle-ball and unfortunately, for growing weeds, dandelions in particular. To my young eyes, dandelions were pretty yellow flowers. In a tender moment as a younger boy I probably even picked a handful of dandelions (pronounced dandy-lions, of course) and offered them to my mother. So it was with no small surprise I learned these "flowers" were not flowers at all, but weeds. No! Dandelions were weeds? I gave my mom *weeds*, not flowers? I knew what weeds were, and what weeds meant: weeding! Dandelions did not look like weeds. They were just too bright and beautiful to be weeds. Who broke the bad news to me? My dad, who approached my brothers and me one Saturday morning, three big empty coffee cans in hand, and offered us a dollar each if we picked all the dandelions in the yard.

Now I say "picked" because that's what I heard. It may be he said "pulled," but to my eight-year-old ears there was no difference. I only remember hearing the word "dollar." My brothers and I each grabbed a can and ran around picking dandelion after dandelion as quickly as we could. That frenetic pace soon gave way to a slower, less enthusiastic approach to the task. This was taking "forever" (although I'm quite sure it wasn't even half-an-hour) and we still had a long way to go. Dad checked on us, and reminded us to stay at it until the job was done. The vision of the dollar had faded and didn't seem like such a big deal anymore. Finally, we had cleared the front of the house, sides and backyard of dandelions. Not a yellow head in sight. We were proud of our work and tired but happy. Dad gave us each a dollar, which helped a lot, and off we went to talk about what we were going to get with all that money.

You can guess what happened the next Saturday morning. With the coffee cans in hand, my dad called us boys together. What was going on? He took us out to the yard and pointed out what I hadn't really noticed—the yard was once again full of dandelions. But this time he did something else; he showed us what it took to get rid of the dandelions once and for all. It wasn't enough just to pick the dandelion, head and stem. We had to dig around the base of each dandelion, get a good grip and carefully but with real effort pull up the entire, unbroken dandelion, root and all. That was the only way to get rid of the weed permanently. Well that was a whole new ball game! It was a relatively quick and easy task to grab the stem of the dandelion and pull off the yellow head, without worrying about the root. It took real work and concentrated effort to get the whole dandelion all at once.

You know what happened. Sometimes, through a combination of luck and focus, I got it right and uprooted the weed. Most of the time, I wasn't so fortunate and ended up breaking off the dandelion somewhere along the root, leaving the rest of it hidden underground, which meant that it would begin growing all over again. I think I began mumbling, "See you next week." The previous Saturday we got bored of the job, but at least we reached our goal, or so we thought. This Saturday was much harder; our hands and knees got dirty and we spent a long time just trying to get one part of the yard cleared. What had seemed like an easy way to earn a dollar was really a tough chore. One thing was for sure, that second Saturday I lost all attraction to dandelions. They were no longer flowers; they were definitely weeds and they were weeds that made my life difficult. Weeds be gone! But that meant a lot of effort and serious focus on uprooting them; if I settled for less, they were going to just keep coming back.

## PLANTING AND SPREADING THE WEEDS

Dandelions are a lot like sin in our lives. Let's be honest, we often sin because it's as attractive as dandelions and seems just as harmless. Sin looks and feels a lot more appealing than doing the right thing. The actual experience of the sinning itself—whether in our thinking, speaking, acting or omitting—is often at first blush and on a surface level very satisfying. We savor the sin and the sinning: *thinking* mean, angry or lustful thoughts; *speaking* gossip or using sarcastic or negative humor; *acting* by watching a degrading movie or spending money frivolously and extravagantly on selfish pursuits; or *omitting* by wasting (I mean "playing") another hour on video games rather than praying or doing something constructive; *avoiding* serving others because it's inconvenient, or *opting out* of involvement in life-giving activities because it wasn't our idea or because we don't get to be the center of attention or in charge. All of these are examples of choosing to do what feels easier, more pleasant or satisfying *in the moment*.

Sin is like that—it's the third (and last!) piece of chocolate cake that I don't need and don't *really* want at one level, but devour anyway. It tastes good in my mouth, but feels like a rock in my stomach five minutes later. The jelly inside the tasty donut of sin is made up of confusion, shame, darkness, disgust and even self-hatred. Sin appears satisfying, but quickly turns sour once I've welcomed it into my life by saying "yes" to it. Sin is never worth what it costs. We get swindled in every sin; we willingly give away something precious and get what is worthless and toxic in return.

Too late do we realize that every sin sinks weed like roots into our lives. Repeat a sin often enough and this weed starts choking the life out of our healthy, virtuous inclinations. The battle of my desires, the fleshly versus the spiritual, intensifies and I lose peace. We've fallen for sin and now pay the price. We get tangled up in the weeds, weeds that looked so much like pretty little flowers at the start. What a mess we make in our lives when we sin!

DIGGING UP THE HIDDEN ROOTS

Confession is an act involving accusing myself for planting and spreading weeds, expressing heartfelt sorrow and even detestation over the many weeds, and asking for God's mercy to give me a fresh start to live a weed-free life. But we are not done yet, we have to go further. God's forgiveness impacts us like what happened on the first Saturday my brothers and I pulled the heads and stems off the dandelions. The grass is cleared of dandelions, but the hidden roots remain. In theological language, forgiveness addresses the *effects* of sin. We have to dig deeper and address the *causes* of sin and deal with the damage caused by our sin. That's where the fourth sentence, "I will make up for it" comes in. If forgiveness addresses the *effects* of sin, it's *penance* that addresses the *causes* of sin. "I will make up for it" expresses the willingness to do penance.

When the priest in Confession gives us a penance, he is pointing us back out into the yard like my dad on that second Saturday. Time to get down to the root causes of these weeds! Leaving Confession forgiven is not the same as experiencing all the healing that Jesus Christ intends for you in this sacrament. The grace poured into our hearts in this sacrament of healing accompanies us back into our lives. Now comes the hard part—rolling up our sleeves, getting down on our hands and knees with pains-taking focus, sober seriousness and persevering patience, and uprooting the causes of sin in our lives. Here is how the *Catechism* makes this point:

> [S]in injures and weakens the sinner himself, as well as his relationships with God and neighbor. Absolution takes away sin, but it does not remedy all the disorders sin has caused. Raised up from sin, the sinner must still recover his full spiritual health by doing something more to make amends for the sin: he must "make satisfaction for" or "expiate" his sins. This satisfaction is also called "penance."(CCC 1459)

In this quote, we see the theological word that is traditionally used for the part of Confession that involves the priest giving us a penance: *satisfaction*. It seems like a strange choice of wording. When we commonly hear and use the word "satisfaction," we think of fulfillment, gratification or contentment. That is not how the word is used in the context of Confession. I remember watching a movie involving 18th century English gentlemen. There was a scene where the antagonist mistreated and humiliated another gentleman who angrily addressed his adversary saying, "I demand satisfaction." He was demanding that his adversary make up for what he had done, that he repair the damage he had caused. Of course, in this case, the adversary repairs the damage by being shot and killed in a duel. In Confession, God does not demand acts of satisfaction out of anger and vengeance, but rather, out of justice and mercy! The *Catechism* brings out the aspect of justice involved in our acts of penance or satisfaction: "Many sins wrong our neighbor. One must do what is possible in order to repair the harm (e.g., return stolen goods, restore the reputation of someone slandered, pay compensation for injuries). Simple justice requires as much." (CCC 1459)

Satisfaction is about "justice", about *making amends* and working to "repair the harm" caused by sin. That's why going to Confession involves not only saying "I did it," "I am sorry" and "Forgive me," but also "I will make up for it." All of a sudden, going to Confession is not the finish line we might have thought it was when it comes to dealing with the sins we've just confessed. These texts make it clear that if we don't intend to say the fourth sentence that will heal our lives, "I will make up for it," then we will not receive all that the Lord is offering to us and asking from us in Confession.

## REPAIRING THE DAMAGE OF SIN

What do I mean when I say that confessing my sins in Confession isn't the finish line? Let me give you an example. Growing up, I played a lot of catch in the backyard with my brothers. I don't know how many times one of us ended up throwing the baseball wildly and breaking a window in the house, but it was more than a few through the years. Whoever did it had to face mom or dad and say, "I did it. I didn't mean to do it. I'm sorry." They would of course be upset that it happened again, but they would always say, "We forgive you. But now you're going to have to take on extra chores to earn the money needed to pay for the window that has to be repaired." My parents certainly forgave whichever of us had broken the window. But there was something that had to be made up for, and that was the damage we caused by our actions.

If we get this point when it comes to our human relationships, why should it be different in our relationship with God? I can receive forgiveness and my sins can be washed away, but that's very different from the damage that sin causes, not just to others, but to myself. When I do penance, I am making up for the damage that I've done to my spiritual state, to my soul. When we say "I will make up for it," we are promising to do whatever is in our power to remedy the brokenness that has come about through our sin. Our sins aren't just a matter of breaking windows. Our sins often break people's hearts, and harden our own.

Let me go further. Satisfaction, doing penance, is not only about justice, it is about *mercy*. Remember, mercy is when God shows us favor when we deserve the opposite. The demand that we do acts of penance is another way that God favors us. Why? Because our acts of penance, when we do them in the right spirit, are done through, with and in Jesus Christ. We never do authentic penance alone. We act in Christ and He acts in us. Our acts of satisfaction are drawn into Jesus Christ' great act of penance, making satisfaction for the sins of the world through His death on the cross. The *Catechism* teaches powerfully on this point:

> Such penances help configure us to Christ, who alone expiated our sins once for all. They allow us to become co-heirs with the risen Christ, "provided we suffer with him." The satisfaction that we make for our sins...is not so much ours as though it were not done through Jesus Christ.

We who can do nothing ourselves, as if just by ourselves, can do all things with the cooperation of "him who strengthens" us. Thus man has nothing of which to boast, but all our boasting is in Christ...in whom we make satisfaction by bringing forth "fruits that befit repentance." These fruits have their efficacy from him, by him they are offered to the Father, and through him they are accepted by the Father. (CCC 1460)

Jesus Christ not only promises to show you mercy by forgiving your sins, His mercy also draws us into His passion and death on the cross. It makes sense. Just as Jesus won the victory over all sin and death by His Passion, death and Resurrection, so also my path to becoming *victorious* over sin (not just *forgiven* of sin) is by being united with Jesus in His Passion, death and Resurrection. Apart from Jesus Christ, we have no ability to have our penance bear the fruit God intends, which is making up for what we've done and re-establishing Christian attitudes in our lives. Because of Him, our acts of penance bear fruit because they pull weeds.

## THE SACRAMENT OF CONFESSION

When I think about my experience of going to Confession as a young man, and compare it to the five sentences that lay out what is asked of me in Confession, the only sentence I was really interested in saying was "Forgive me." That's the sentence I wanted to begin and end with because that was what I wanted most of all from Confession; I just wanted to be forgiven. While it is so critical to apply God's remedy for the *effects* of sin by going to Confession, the sacrament itself also asks that we apply God's remedy for the *causes* of sin in our lives. That's what the fourth sentence, "I will make up for it," is all about. If we don't uproot the causes of our sinful actions, the sins will resurface.

The *Catechism* teaches us about the penance given by the priest in Confession:

> The *penance* the confessor imposes must take into account the penitent's personal situation and must seek his spiritual good. It must correspond as far as possible with the gravity and nature of the sins committed. It can consist of prayer, an offering, works of mercy, service of neighbor, voluntary self-denial, sacrifices, and above all the patient acceptance of the cross we must bear. (CCC 1460)

For too many Catholics, the penance they receive in Confession is not something they think much about. Say your assigned prayers and go home. It doesn't seem like such a big deal. The penance all by itself is rarely significant enough to uproot sin from our lives. Why do I say that? Because oftentimes, the penance that many of us receive is not very difficult or extensive: "Say two *Our Fathers* and three *Hail Marys.*" That would be okay if we Catholics today had a solid understanding of the importance of penance for our spiritual lives, and made ongoing, intentional efforts to live a life that incorporated penance. Simply put, we don't. If we did, we would be able to take the penance offered us in Confession, even if it was only reciting a small number of *Our Fathers,* and fruitfully use that time to discern other acts of penance that would make up for what we've done and help uproot the causes of sin in our lives. What might those acts be?

Think of a penance that "correspond[s]...with the... nature of the sins committed." In fact, this is more likely the type of penance you would receive when you go to Confession today. Let's look at some sample penances that correspond to particular sins: For the proud person: "Take some time thanking God for the blessings He has given you." For the person too busy to pray: "Take five to ten minutes right after Confession and sit quietly in the presence of Our Lord." For the person who speaks in hurtful ways to his wife: "Say something positive or affirming to her every day this week." These are helpful penances; they point us back to our lives and offer a concrete action or set of actions that might gain some momentum and help us address those stubborn, weed-like sins in our spiritual lives.

## GETTING INTO SPIRITUAL SHAPE

St. Philip Neri was a great saint with a reputation for being full of joy. He lived in Rome in the 16th century at the time of the Protestant Reformation and the Catholic Counter Reformation. There's a story about a woman who confessed to him an ongoing sin of gossip. St. Philip Neri gave her absolution. Before he announced her penance, he took her to the top of his church, gave her a feather pillow and asked her to rip it open and empty it of feathers. As you can imagine, the feathers went in every direction. Then, for her penance, St. Philip asked her to go pick up all the scattered feathers. Her face probably froze and her response was probably something like, "What? What are you talking about? That is impossible!" I don't know if St. Philip made her try anyway, but his message was clear: when you gossip, you don't have control over what happens to your words once you release them. They scatter in every direction and can cause irreparable harm. Gathering up those feathers would be like trying to take back the words this woman spoke. The connection between the form of the penance and the nature of the sin is clear. So also is the connection between the severity of the sin and the penance. But that was then. We are here now. If other ages of the church are sometimes critiqued for being overly harsh on penitential practices and the doing of penance, that is not our problem today.

Our moment in history is soft when it comes to giving penances, and even more in doing penance. In fact, even a mention of embracing practices of self-denial for the sake of spiritual growth is looked upon by some people as unhealthy and an attempt to return to a bygone age of excesses in self-discipline. Because our age is at one extreme—that of avoiding penance and talk about penance—we are not good at striking a balance in understanding penance. Propose moving back toward a middle ground and get ready to have your suggestion labeled as going to the opposite extreme. I call it pendulum thinking; thinking that can see only two positions, the current position and the extreme opposite. Ironically, millions of people in secular settings today embrace all kinds of self-denial and self-discipline in pursuit of physical "perfection." Plans involving serious commitments to dieting and exercise are applauded, but similar planning and efforts for spiritual growth are much more rare. If our moment is at one extreme, where do we find an expression that addresses spiritual growth in association with penance that is more balanced? One place we can look is to St. John of the Cross, whose writings on the spiritual life have deeply influenced subsequent ages in the history of the Catholic Church. What follows is a comment by Hans Urs von Balthasar on one of St. John's great works, the *Ascent of Mt. Carmel:*

According to the *Ascent*, Book 1, Chapter 13, the foundation of all spiritual life is 'the habitual desire to imitate Christ in all things' by 'mortification and renunciation of self for the love of Christ, who in his life on earth had no other gratification, nor desired any other, than the fulfillment of his Father's will, which he called his meat and food.' And this mortification begins with the active choice and preference of 'the more difficult' instead of 'the easier' and 'the less pleasant' instead of the gratifying, of 'the unconsoling' instead of the consoling, of 'the lowest and most despised' instead of the higher and more precious—in short, of 'total poverty in all the things of this world.'[1]

We probably haven't heard too many homilies or talks that developed a vision of what it meant to imitate Christ along those lines! If anything, you probably had to read the passage a couple of times to be sure you read what you did. Choosing the difficult and "less pleasant" over the "easier" and more "gratifying"? How many of us live according to that standard? I hate to admit that my "active choice and preference" are much more inclined toward the easier and more gratifying. How many see "total poverty in all the things of this world" as the ideal that is not meant

---

1. Hans Urs von Balthasar, *The Glory of the Lord: A Theological Aesthetics Vol. III* (San Francisco: Ignatius Press, 1982), 162.

just for cloistered religious, but as something that even we lay people should strive to live out in our own way? I like being independent and self-sufficient. Encountering my radical need for God and my utter incapacity to honor Him without His grace—that is not naturally attractive to me. Where on my list of desires is doing the will of God the Father—before or after making sure I get to watch my favorite TV show? All it takes is a few quotes from one section in St. John of the Cross to convict me (and hopefully the age in which we live) to stop and seriously ask whether I have taken proper account of the importance of penance in my spiritual life.

## EMBRACING A LIFE OF PENANCE

After the Council of Trent in the sixteenth century, Catholic universities and seminaries began to systematize the way theology was taught. Over time, a series of manuals or treatises was developed, with each manual covering a significant theme or subject in Catholic theology. At times, manuals linked together two themes, like "God is One" and "God is Three," or "Faith" and "Reason." This method of teaching theology lost favor in many places after the second Vatican Council. Even so, there was a profound insight involved in how the manuals taught about growth in the spiritual life. The manual that covered spiritual growth and maturity linked together in its title two themes that went hand in hand.

The manual was called *Ascetical Theology and Mystical Theology*. *Ascetical* comes from a Greek word that means "training." In simplistic terms, ascetical theology examined the Church's teaching on the what, why and how to train ourselves to deny ourselves and live for God (called *asceticism*) and how to "put to death" the fallen inclinations of the "flesh" in our lives (called *mortification*). Mystical theology explored the traditional stages of spiritual development and the gifts and graces of the Holy Spirit that God granted to those seeking to grow spiritually. The coupling of these two themes, *Ascetical Theology and Mystical Theology* highlights a point that our culture tends to obscure. What point?

In our Catholic tradition, you will not reach the heights of holiness without embracing a life of penance. This means embracing a life of self-denial as well as embracing your cross every day. We want spiritual growth. We even hunger for spiritual experiences. What we don't hear mentioned often or would like to leave to the side is asceticism and mortification. I believe there are not as many mystics today because there are not as many ascetics today. Mysticism without asceticism is the slogan for today. What it leads to is (the chase for) spiritual experiences without (resulting in) spiritual maturity. What can we do about it? Learn to live a life that involves penance.

# LIVING A (CONFESSIONAL) LIFE
# OF PENANCE

St. Thomas Aquinas states in the Third Part of the *Summa Theologica*, "[that] by satisfaction [acts of penance], we are destroying our sins altogether." He goes on to say that "satisfaction uproots the causes of sin" which he identifies as three: concupiscence of the flesh, concupiscence of the eyes and the pride of life. *Prayer* overcomes the pride of life because through prayer we are humbling ourselves. We are submitting to God and acknowledging Him as our Lord and the master of our lives. *Fasting* is a way of diminishing concupiscence of the flesh, that pull towards sins of the body including lust, pornography, adultery and gluttony. *Almsgiving* is a way of weakening and uprooting the concupiscence of the eyes that makes us look at the goods of this world and desire them over God. God graces us to do penance in union with Jesus Christ in order to uproot sin and help clear it from our lives. It would take another book to examine these three themes in any depth, so I've decided to focus on one of the three forms of penance, the one that gets the least attention and is the most misunderstood: fasting. For the remainder of this chapter, I offer some reflections on what fasting is, why it's important and how we can embrace fasting as an integral part of our spiritual lives today.

## FASTING AS A MEANS TO ENCOUNTER CHRIST

You might be thinking, isn't fasting something the Catholic Church has cut back on since Vatican II? Shouldn't we do the same? Sounds like it could be harmful to my health if I'm not careful. True enough, so always fast with care. But fast! Here is what Paul VI identified as benefits associated with fasting, in a document released *after* Vatican II:

> One fasts or applies physical discipline to "chastise one's own soul," to "humble oneself in the sight of his own God," to "turn one's face toward Jehovah," to "dispose oneself to prayer," to "understand" more intimately the things which are divine, or to prepare oneself for the encounter with God.[2]

Who would have guessed that fasting could lead to a more intimate knowledge of God, by removing blockages to, and preparing you for, an encounter with God? Fasting is not dieting, though your fasting may incorporate a decision to diet. Just to be clear, fasting is not going without food entirely, or eating just bread and water. Fasting is based on sufficiency. When you fast, the Church proposes

---

2. Paul VI, Apostolic Constitution on Fast and Abstinence *Paenitimini* (17 February 1966) §17–22 www.vatican va/holy_father/paul_vi/apost_constitutions/documents/hf_p-vi_apc_19660217_paenitimini_en.html

that you eat what is *sufficient* for your situation in life. An offensive lineman on a football team is probably going to be eating a lot more on a day he is fasting than I will on an ordinary day. Fasting is about eating what is *sufficient* rather than what *satisfies*. The Church proposes that this is equal to one full meal and two partial meals that don't equal another full meal. It ordinarily involves abstaining from meat. The Catholic Church *requires* fasting from us only on Ash Wednesday and Good Friday.* The Church *recommends* fasting and abstinence much more than that. Why? Here is a list of statements I believe are truths about fasting:

1. You will not understand the power of fasting until you fast. Reading about it will never suffice.

2. You will not realize the depth of your attachment to food until you fast.

3. You will not be convinced of the strength of those attachments to food and know how weak you are to resist them until you fast...and fail.

4. You will not realize that by satisfying your desire for food, you cover over and sometimes smother your deeper desires for God and for spiritual things. You will

---

* There are certain exceptions to the fasting requirement. For example, those younger than 18 years and those older than 60 years are exempt.

realize it once you begin restraining yourself from satisfying those desires through fasting.

5. You will not realize that fasting is the weapon of the powerless. When you are faced with worldly situations and spiritual attacks that are beyond your strength, fast. When you do, God's power will become manifest and clear a path to freedom for you.

6. Fasting diminishes and clears away so much that deadens our spiritual lives.

7. You won't be convinced about the correctness of these statements until you've actually made a serious effort to incorporate fasting into your spiritual life.

## TIPS TO SUCCESSFUL FASTING

Here are some insights and practical tips to remember about embracing fasting as a penance:

1. Don't be surprised that on the day you fast, you find yourself complaining internally by lunchtime at least (or maybe at the latest!). You may even be thinking to yourself, "I'm never going to make it! God can't want this for me!" even though you haven't made much of a change in your eating for that day. A lot of what happens in fasting is in your head as much as your body.

2. Choose to fast in a way that involves a real sacrifice or challenge, but not one that will weigh so heavily on you that it's too much for you. For example, on a day of fasting, drink tea rather than coffee, or less coffee without

cream or sugar. If you eat breakfast, choose to eat something that will nourish you without necessarily satisfying you (e.g. oatmeal instead of a bagel with cream cheese or a donut).

3. Fast intentionally, that is, with a plan. Don't just float into your day of fasting. Think through and plan *when, what, how much, where* and *with whom* you are going to eat. Don't set yourself up for failure!

4. Replace some of the time you would have spent eating in prayer, especially reading your Bible. When Jesus was tempted in the desert by the devil after fasting for 40 days, He said that man did not live on bread alone but on every word that comes from the mouth of God. Consider the reading of Scripture as a form of nourishing your spirit. Fasting is traditionally connected with prayer.

5. Take the money and time you save through fasting and put it at the service of a good cause. This connects your fasting in some way to almsgiving. We do this in Lent when we put the money we've saved from eating differently into a special collection for those who are poor and hungry in the world.

6. Don't stay up until midnight on a Friday in Lent and then eat a large meatball sub with chips and a coke. I speak as one with authority, because I did that one year. As the clock struck midnight, I took the largest bite I could manage of that sub. Let's just say that this was not a good example of correct fasting. I followed the letter of the law,

but missed out on the spirit of it, and got a big stomach ache to boot.

7. Don't expect fasting to ever get easy, but expect that the difficulties you face in fasting will become acceptable. We will see over time that our ability to restrain ourselves from eating increases. It's a bit like making the effort to clean your garage or closet. The first time you tackle it is the most difficult. Other times are still difficult, but the difficulties are not a surprise anymore. This helps tremendously. You have walked through the cleaning process before and even might remember how good you felt when you finished. Fasting is like that.

8. While I have only mentioned fasting from food, fasting can also take on many other forms: fasting from talking negatively, watching television, using the internet, playing video games or fasting from sins you may struggle with.

9. You might also fast from "choosing what is easy or comfortable" (remember the quote from St. John of the Cross?). This might involve little acts of penance like sitting in a less comfortable chair or sitting up straight rather than sitting back comfortably in your chair. St. John might invite you to try kneeling at your dinner table when you eat your meal or to sleep on the floor rather than your bed. We realize pretty quickly how much we rely on what is comfortable and easy.

10. Fast as a means of addressing a social evil, like abortion. Remember, fasting is the weapon of the powerless. God moves in power when we fast and pray. There are pro-life efforts that promote regular fasting or even fasting for 40 days in imitation of Jesus as a means of saving babies' lives, rescuing women from the devastation of abortion and converting hearts and minds to a pro-life mentality.

11. If you are serious about incorporating fasting into your spiritual life, then seek out good counsel, preferably from a trained spiritual director. I know there are not enough spiritual directors to meet all our needs, so just make sure you are not fasting in a hidden way. Don't let the world know you are fasting, but do let someone who is spiritually mature know, so you don't rely only on your own discernment about what is healthy and appropriate.

12. Whatever form of fasting you engage in, please remember that the key to all acts of penance are that they are to be done in union with Jesus Christ. All of our acts of satisfaction are to be offered up and drawn into His perfect act of satisfaction, His death on the cross.

Through penance, whether by prayer, fasting or almsgiving, we are uprooting the causes of sin that remain hidden even after we've been healed of the effects of sin by being forgiven. Once forgiven, we take steps that say, "I am serious, I will make up for it." But how committed are we to walk the path of holiness God establishes for our lives? The fifth sentence that will heal your life will answer that question. When it comes to sin, are you ready to say, "I will never do it again"?

# CHAPTER SEVEN

# RESOLUTION: I WILL NEVER DO IT AGAIN

*Primarily, God is not bound to punish sin;*
*He is bound to destroy sin.*
*The only vengeance worth having on sin*
*is to make the sinner himself*
*its executioner.*

George MacDonald

I remember my first car. A 1974 Mercury Montego I bought used...and it showed. It was lemon-yellow in color and a lemon in other ways as well. I always had a difficult time getting the car to pass the required yearly state inspection. Something always needed to be fixed, and that meant money for repairs. I dreaded the annual trip to the car inspection station. Getting a "Rejected" sticker meant I had ten days to have the car repaired, or get fined and fined some more until the car passed inspection. I found the whole process frustrating. I didn't want to face all the time, runarounds and expense involved in getting the car to make the grade. So there was a pretty good chance my inspection sticker would expire. When I eventually got the colored inspection sticker put on the inside corner of the windshield, it was a huge relief.

One year, after my inspection sticker expired, a policeman pulled me over and gave me a ticket for not having an up-to-date sticker. You would think I would learn my lesson and deal with it right away, but I was too busy to make time for it. I thought of another option—make my own "inspection sticker" until I could find the time to get around to it. I figured out what color the inspection stickers were that year, found colored paper that matched it and cut out a piece of paper and put it where the inspection sticker was supposed to go. This was the condition of my car when I entered the seminary in my junior year of college.

One of the recommended practices in the seminary was regular Confession. Every two weeks I would dutifully go to Confession, normally to the same priest. The first few times I went, I would bring up my inspection sticker issue and confess that I was not honoring the law. The third or fourth time I brought this up in Confession, the priest began to offer me his counsel after I finished confessing my sins. Regarding my inspection sticker, he said, "Tom, stop confessing that." I was thinking, "Yeesss! I'm off the hook!" He closed down that line of thinking with his next sentence, "Stop confessing that sin until you are willing to do something about it." Ouch. Those words stung me to the heart. I was convicted. Believe me, by my next Confession two weeks later my car had passed inspection.

What was lacking in my previous Confessions that I discovered in this Confession? Let's follow the path of the five sentences: I was confessing my sins every time—I said "I did it." I was also sorry. I asked for forgiveness. I was willing to make up for it, in the sense that I would do the penance the priest gave me. What was lacking was the last sentence associated with Confession that will heal my life, "I will never do it again." I was not determined to eliminate that sinful situation from my life. Instead, I was nonchalant about getting the inspection sticker taken care of, and time passed and I forgot about it until the next Confession. My basic issue was a lack of full contrition.

I have already defined contrition as sorrow of soul and the detestation of sins. I had that in some measure. But there is an element in contrition I haven't discussed yet. The *Catechism* teaches that contrition includes one other critical aspect, "the resolution not to sin again" (CCC 1451). If we want "a more personal encounter with the crucified forgiving Christ" (Pope John Paul II, *Redeemer of Man*, 20), then we must be ready to live out the last of the five sentences once we leave the confessional: "I will never do it again." When we walk away from Confession, we need a firm, courageous resolve not to sin ever again. Any sin. Ever. It shows up as zeal for honoring God and for personal holiness present in saints like St. Dominic Savio.

## DEATH BUT NOT SIN!

St. Dominic was born in Turin, Italy in 1842. He lived a short life of extraordinary holiness until he died of a lung disease, possibly tuberculosis, at the age of fourteen. When he made his First Communion at the age of seven, he wrote down four promises to himself that he kept in a little book and read over and over. They were maxims for his life. His fourth maxim read: "Death but not sin." That's resolve! Make that the motto for your life and then see what happens as you strive to live it out. Sadly, we are not as bold or resolute as St. Dominic. If we examined our own lives and had to come up with a motto that fittingly described how we actually lived, it would probably read something like this: "Discomfort but not sin." Once things get too uncomfortable or difficult, our resolve weakens and we settle for less; we sin. At least I do, more often than I want to admit. To say, "I will never sin again. I would rather die than sin," seems utterly unrealistic and beyond me. Is God trying so set me up for failure? Why would He ask me to strive to live out a sentence that seems impossible?

With the fifth and final sentence that will heal your life—I will never do it again—we reach the pinnacle of difficulty. I mentioned earlier in the book that each of the five sentences strikes me as more difficult to live than the one before it. All the other four sentences—I did it. I am sorry. Forgive me. I will make up for it—seemed difficult when we considered them one at a time. But compared to the challenge of living out this last sentence, those other four pale in comparison. How can I possibly say "I will never do it again" and mean it? I am only human after all! What does God expect? That is a very good question. What *does* God expect? Do you know? If we don't know, we better find out.

## GO AND SIN NO MORE

Do you remember the passage from Scripture, "Go and sin no more"? It's found in the Gospel of John 8:11, where Jesus is speaking with the woman caught in adultery. The woman was brought before Jesus by the scribes and the Pharisees, who told Him that the woman was caught in the act of adultery, and that according to the Law of Moses she was to be stoned. They wanted Jesus' counsel about what they should do. At least, that's what they claimed. In reality, they were setting a trap for Jesus, to see if He would defy the Law of Moses so they could bring a charge against Him. Jesus doesn't reply. He bends down and begins to write on the ground. Then He addresses the gathered crowd, saying that the one among them without sin should cast the first stone. When He looks up, the people are all gone and Jesus is alone with the woman. He doesn't condemn her, He forgives her. But what does He say to her last of all? Jesus doesn't say, "Go try your best." He doesn't say, "Go and sin only twice a day," or "Go and sin only occasionally." No, He tells her "Go and sin no more." Not a lot of wiggle room there. Don't just avoid this particular sin, avoid ALL sin. What is ironic is that Jesus tells her to sin no more right after he asked the gathered crowd whether any of them was without sin! No one dared to step forward and claim to be without sin. Yet He commands this woman to sin no more. What is going on?

Scripture makes it clear that sin is not something we should ever settle for as God's children. One reason some sins remain in our lives is because we choose to let them be there. Look at Sirach 15: 14–20:

> When God, in the beginning, created man, he made him subject to his own free choice. If you choose you can keep the commandments; it is loyalty to do his will. There are set before you fire and water; to whichever you choose, stretch forth your hand. Before man are life and death, which-ever he chooses shall be given him. Immense is the

wisdom of the Lord; he is mighty in power, and all-seeing. The eyes of God see all he has made; he understands man's every deed. No man does he command to sin, to none does he give strength for lies.

What about when sinful temptations overwhelm us? Even then, when we are tempted to sin, we still have choice. God offers us the grace to defeat temptations and faithfully make it through trials of faith: "No trial has come to you but what is human. God is faithful and will not let you be tried beyond your strength; but with the trial he will also provide a way out, so that you may be able to bear it" (1 Cor. 10:13). When Christ says, "sin no more" He is not setting us up for failure. He is raising our eyes to the heights of holiness to which we are called as God's children:

> Like obedient children, do not act in compliance with the desires of your former ignorance but, as he who called you is holy, *be holy yourselves in every aspect of your conduct,* for it is written, "Be holy because I (am) holy. Now if you invoke as Father him who judges impartially according to each one's works, conduct yourselves with reverence during the time of your sojourning, realizing that *you were ransomed from your futile conduct,* handed on by your ancestors, not with perishable

things like silver or gold but *with the precious blood of Christ* as of a spotless unblemished lamb. (1 Peter 1:14–15) *(emphasis mine)*

The last part of that passage gives us some insight into what it cost Jesus to set us free from sin. He chose death because we had chosen sin. Shouldn't we choose death rather than sin? He chose to die to free us from sin. Shouldn't we choose to live free from sin? St. Dominic had it right. At seven years of age, he got it right. Why don't we? We need greater resolve!

## THE PERFECTION OF CHARITY

If we are going to live out a resolution to sin no more, we need it to be based in a God-given vision for our lives. Otherwise, it will only be frustrating at least, and potentially inflate our pride at worst, if we think that sinning no more is the result of our own efforts. Jesus gives us a vision of perfection for our lives in the Sermon on the Mount when He states, "So be perfect, just as your heavenly Father is perfect."

When we read that sentence, it is easy to get overwhelmed. Jesus is not only saying that I must be perfect, which is already beyond me, but I must be perfect "as my heavenly Father is perfect." How perfect is that? Infinitely perfect. Perfect in a way that divinity is perfect. Absolutely, completely, eternally perfect, without growth or diminishment. How can I, a human being, a created being, approach that type of perfection? On my own, there is no way at all. Once again in this book we are face-to-face with a confession of faith. As we consider our call to holiness, we confess God's infinite holiness and confess our misery, and we confess God's perfection and our poverty to fulfill the call of Christ. This is our confession of faith. This is living a confessional life. When we examine our lives, it is obvious to anyone with a modicum of self-awareness that we do not live perfect lives every day or even any day. Does this undermine the Scripture and the command to "go and sin no more" and "be perfect as your heavenly Father is perfect"? Is the resolution not to sin again an ultimately frustrating resolution? On our own, the answer is yes, but we are not asked to be perfect on our own strength.

The only way we can fulfill the command to be perfect after the manner of perfection of our heavenly Father is by participating in His divine life, by having a share in His holiness. The Good News of our Catholic faith is that we do share in God's own divine life through the filial adoption that is given to us in Baptism. Because of that union in love, won for us by Jesus Christ, we receive the power to live in accord with our call to perfection. The *Catechism of the Catholic Church* confirms this idea:

> He who believes in Christ becomes a son of God. This filial adoption transforms him by

giving him the ability to follow the example of Christ. It makes him capable of acting rightly and doing good. *In union with his Savior, the disciple attains the perfection of charity which is holiness.* Having matured in grace, the moral life blossoms into eternal life in the glory of heaven. (1709) *(emphasis mine)*

We are re-created as adopted sons and daughters of the Father in the sacraments of initiation. God's Holy Spirit dwells in us. What is inconceivable apart from God's sanctifying grace becomes possible through His Holy Spirit. The *Catechism of the Catholic Church* points us to the sacraments as sources of God's strength:

The sacraments of Christian initiation— Baptism, Confirmation, and the Eucharist—lay the *foundations* of every Christian life. "The sharing in the divine nature given to men through the grace of Christ bears a certain likeness to the origin, development, and nourishing of natural life. The faithful are born anew by Baptism, strengthened by the sacrament of Confirmation, and receive in the Eucharist the food of eternal life. By means of these sacraments of Christian initiation, they thus receive in increasing measure the treasures of the divine life and advance toward the perfection of charity." (1212)

In these two quotes, the *Catechism* introduces a very important and traditional phrase that provides us with a key to understanding the call to be perfect. The phrase is "perfection of charity." In our tradition, that phrase has been used when interpreting our call to be perfect as our heavenly Father is perfect:

> "All Christians in any state or walk of life are called to the fullness of Christian life and to the perfection of charity." All are called to holiness: "Be perfect, as your heavenly Father is perfect." In order to reach this perfection the faithful should use the strength dealt out to them by Christ's gift, so that...doing the will of the Father in everything, they may wholeheartedly devote themselves to the glory of God and to the service of their neighbor. (CCC 2013)

We share in God's perfection through the gift of love (in Latin, *caritas*, translated here as "charity") that God communicates to us in the sacraments. St. Thomas Aquinas, in the *Summa Theologica* helps us take the next step in understanding the perfection of charity when he connects it with the first and greatest Commandment: "You must love the Lord your God with your whole heart, your whole soul, your whole mind and your whole strength." The call to the perfection of charity is the call to love God perfectly with every dimension of our being.

St. Thomas goes further and introduces two different ways that we attain the perfection of charity. The first is by loving the Lord your God *as much as you are able to love Him.* St. Thomas states that this form of the perfection of charity is only attainable for those who are in Heaven. Why? Because here on earth we still struggle with human weakness and sin. We will only attain that perfection when we reach Heaven. When we attain the perfection God plans for us in Heaven, we will be able to love God perfectly.

What about on earth? St. Thomas teaches that while we are here on earth we are sojourners, people who are on the way home, people who have not yet arrived. The call to the perfection of charity for those of us still on the way is different than what we will be capable of in Heaven. Here, I still live in a fallen world where sin abounds, and I am impacted by that reality; I am weak and prone to sin. At the same time, Christ has won the victory over sin and death and He is also at work in me, so I have His strength to be victorious over sin. Here is the battle we face on earth, between the desires of the flesh and the desires of the spirit!

## FALLING INTO SIN OR JUMPING INTO SIN?

The call to the perfection of charity in this world that is fallen but redeemed, still rings out as a call to "Sin no more," and asks for our courageous resolve (I will never do it again!). But it does so with the realization that Christ's victory in my life is not complete and will not be complete until I am in Heaven. I will *fall* into sin. What I must not do is *jump* into sin. There is a difference between falling into sin and jumping into sin. What do I mean?

One day, Kari and I had all our kids down at a local beach south of Seattle. We were enjoying a stroll, dressed in shorts, pants, shoes and socks. I bring up that detail because of what happened next. My two young sons, John Mark and John Luke, three and two years old respectively, both got soaking wet from head to toe. But they ended up in the water through very different paths. John Mark fell into the water. John Luke jumped into the water. They were both wet, but John Mark got wet accidentally; he wasn't paying attention, lost his balance and fell in. John Luke on the other hand, saw the inviting look of the water and he wanted to get wet, even though Kari and I had both sternly told him not to get wet and to stay out of the water. Despite our prohibitions, at the right moment he broke free from holding my hand and ran as fast as he could out into the shallow water. There is all the difference in the world between what happened to John Mark and John Luke. John Mark got wet without willing it. It was an accident. He lost his balance. John Luke knew that it was wrong to get wet, broke free from my hand willfully and ran into the water, all the while ignoring our shouted protests.

While on earth, we will always have to deal with the reality of stumbling and falling into sin because of human weakness that is part of the human condition. How many times do you sin, not because you've given it a lot of thought or made a conscious decision to disobey God, but you just slipped up in your thinking or speech and then caught yourself afterwards? "There I go again! Why do I do that?" That's falling into sin. St. Thomas teaches that sinning like that is not contrary to the perfection of charity. It is not contrary to Jesus' requirement that we be perfect as our heavenly Father is perfect. It is not contrary to Jesus' statement to the woman and to us, "Go and sin no more." It is not contrary to a resolve that says "I will never do it again." It is a humbling situation we are in while we are on earth. We will continue to fall into sin out of human weakness until the day we go home to God, when we will attain the perfection of charity perfectly!

What is contrary to the perfection of charity attainable by us here on earth is jumping into sin. Choosing to sin. Intentionally breaking free from union with the Lord who takes us by the hand to lead us on the path of holiness. What is contrary is choosing not to listen to the protests of conscience that tell us to stay out of sinful situations and disobedient actions. When we do that we are refusing to love the Lord our God with all our hearts, souls, minds and strength.

We are called to be perfect as our heavenly Father is perfect and one day we will be there with Him in Heaven. On earth, living the perfection of charity means loving the Lord our God with all our heart, soul, mind and strength, and never choosing to disobey what our heavenly Father commands. We all recognize that we stumble and fall and will continue to do so. We just shouldn't jump!

You have heard the famous maxim, "Christians aren't perfect, just forgiven." That gets it partly right. We Christians are called to be perfect with the perfection that is possible here on earth. That doesn't mean we will never disobey the Lord. It means we should never willingly choose to remain in a situation where we settle for less than God's standard of holiness for our lives. What is that standard? That we "be holy in every aspect of our conduct," as it says in 1 Peter. What was I doing when I would confess the sin of not getting my car inspected and falsifying the sticker? I was willingly choosing to remain in the situation that was not honoring God or His call to holiness for my life. When you fall into sin, get up and clean yourself off by making a humble Confession. When you jump into sin, get up and clean yourself off by making a contrite Confession, including the resolve to say, "I will never do that again." That would be perfect!

In the next chapter, we'll explore how we strengthen our resolve to "never sin again" through making a regular Confession. A regular Confession is a practice that makes perfect. Here, we are going to look at how proper preparation for Confession is the key to accessing the healing grace that awaits us in the sacrament. Proper preparation makes perfect through an effective examination of conscience.

## THE EXAMINATION OF CONSCIENCE AND THE SACRAMENT OF CONFESSION

One morning I was traveling to the main studio of Sacred Heart Radio to do my daily radio program. Normally I host the radio program from the studio at my office, but this day I had some meetings in the area where the main studio is located, about thirty miles away. I had been to the headquarters of Sacred Heart radio a number of times, so I wasn't worried about getting lost. I should have been paying more attention, however, because I took a wrong turn. I recognized almost immediately I had gone down the wrong road, so I reversed direction and got back on the right road. I was never really lost, but I did take a wrong turn.

What would have really helped me was a GPS, a global positioning system that you find available now in many newer cars. You may have one, or have ridden in a car with one in it. Before starting out on a trip, you input your destination into the system, and then sit back and listen for directions. It lets you know when a turn is coming and if you make a wrong turn, the system speaks to you, "Wrong turn. In one hundred yards, turn around." Yes, I could have used a GPS system on that morning. I wouldn't have made the wrong turn, because I would have been listening for the system to tell me when to turn. I would have stayed on the right road, as long as I listened.

As I was thinking about my need for a GPS, it struck me that I do have a GPS, but it's not in my car. For many of us striving to live as followers of Jesus Christ, our problem is not that we get completely lost or off track. What is more likely is that we take a wrong turn in our thinking, speaking or acting and have to "turn around" (the root meaning of the word "repent" is "to turn around"). All human beings have a built in, internal GPS system that tells us when we are approaching a crossroads and lets us know which way to turn. When we make a wrong turn, it also lets us know. Our internal GPS system is called our conscience. I have already brought up the concept of conscience in previous chapters, identifying it as the voice within you that you hear as your own voice that is not your own. It is the voice of God within you. But what does it mean to "examine" our conscience?

## HEAR THE VOICE OF GOD

Every year or so I make an appointment to see my doctor. It's time for my physical examination. The doctor does a variety of things to get a clear picture of what's happening inside of me. She looks in my ears and mouth, measures my blood pressure. But when it comes time to examine my heart, she has to listen. She asks me to be still and quiet and then she uses her stethoscope to listen intently to my heart. That's a lot like what is required from us when we examine our conscience. Remember that your conscience is found in the center of your being, in what Scripture and our Tradition call the heart. Listening to the voice of God at work within conscience requires of us some discipline. We must be still and quiet and listen with focused attention on what emerges from our hearts. If I am going to make a good examination of conscience, I need to give myself sufficient time (at least 15–30 minutes) and put myself in a position where I can listen (that means not in a room with easily-accessible distractions like a computer or a television). In that place of solitude and silence, I am better able to listen to the voice of God that speaks in the depths of my heart. The *Catechism of the Catholic Church* teaches us how important it is to be able to reflect on what is happening deep within us if we hope to make a good examination of conscience:

> It is important for every person to be sufficiently present to himself in order to hear and follow the voice of his conscience. This requirement of *interiority* is all the more necessary as life often distracts us from any reflection, self-examination or introspection: "Return to your conscience, question

it...Turn inward, brethren, and in everything you do, see God as your witness." (1779)

An examination of conscience is our opportunity to stop and reflect on our lives and to ask, "God how have you been at work in my day? God, where were you today?" Or even, "God, help me recognize if I made any wrong turns today."

## PREPARING FOR CONFESSION

In order to receive all the benefits that the healing sacrament of Confession offers, we must make a good examination of conscience prior to going to Confession. We also find this taught to us in the *Catechism*, along with some recommended aids for making one:

> The reception of this sacrament ought to be prepared for by an *examination of conscience* made in the light of the Word of God. The passages best suited to this can be found in the Ten Commandments, the moral catechesis of the Gospels and the apostolic Letters, such as the Sermon on the Mount and the apostolic teachings. (CCC 1454)

The *Catechism* recommends that our examination of conscience be made in the light of God's Word. When we seek His voice in the Scriptures, it will enlighten what is happening in our hearts. Prayerfully reading God's Word is a powerful way to examine our conscience. Why? Hebrews 4:12–13 gives us the answer:

> Indeed, the word of God is living and effective, sharper than any two-edged sword, penetrating even between soul and spirit, joints and marrow, and able to discern reflections and thoughts of the heart. No creature is concealed from him, but everything is naked and exposed to the eyes of him to whom we must render an account.

When we read the Scriptures suggested by the *Catechism* as part of our examination of conscience, we are inviting the majestic light of God's holiness to shine a bright light on our daily lives, our thoughts, words, deeds and omissions. By doing this, we will be able to identify those areas in our lives where we have failed to honor God and need to confess. I encourage you to use the *Catechism of the Catholic Church* as an aid in examining your conscience if you haven't done so in a while.

The *Catechism* also suggests that our examination of conscience be made with reference to the Ten Commandments. The Church teaches in accord with the Scriptures that the natural law, the law of God written in our hearts, comes to expression in the Ten Commandments. The voice of God at work in conscience illuminates our lives in light of the Ten Commandments.

It's like an internal GPS system God gives—He has written the Commandments on our hearts, and His voice within us helps us realize when we've taken a wrong turn and need to turn around and get back on the right path. When we hear that voice telling us to turn around and we act accordingly, we experience conversion.

## EXAMINATION OF CONSCIENCE AS A DAILY PRACTICE

What will help you become accustomed to making a good examination of conscience in preparation for Confession is to incorporate a regular, even daily, practice of examining your conscience. I learned one form of this practice when I was in the seminary from a wise Jesuit spiritual director. It involved setting aside about ten to fifteen minutes or so at the end of your day. Begin by addressing God in prayer, asking Him for the grace of enlightenment as you examine your conscience, and then take three steps: 1) identify through quiet reflection all the ways you recognized and responded to God's presence and action in your day, and then give thanks to God for that; 2) identify through quiet reflection all the ways you either failed to recognize or failed to respond to God's presence and action in your day, and then repent and ask God for forgiveness; and 3) make a resolution that tomorrow you will recognize and respond to God more completely than you did today. If you are willing to take on this spiritual discipline, you will become more aware of God's voice at work in your conscience.

Learning how to make a good examination of conscience is a key to discovering the ways that we settle for sin in our lives. More importantly, it will help us grow in our desire and resolve to say and mean the fifth sentence that will heal our lives, "I will never do it again."

## LIVING A CONFESSIONAL LIFE

When my wife Kari and I were first married, we lived in Washington, D.C. where I was completing my doctoral program in systematic theology at Catholic University. In the late nineties, we relocated to the Seattle area where Kari grew up. One Friday evening in August, soon after moving west, Kari took me downtown to see the beautiful Seattle waterfront and the famous Pike Place Market. While casually strolling down one of the side streets, we passed by a well-known Irish pub. Kari wanted me to see it so we went in to take a look. Within seconds of entering the bar, someone came up to Kari with a big smile and said "Kari DeLorenzo, it's great to see you!" We were surprised to say the least. What a coincidence that we should bump into someone who knew Kari. All of a sudden, a few other men and women came over and similarly addressed Kari by her maiden name. She was as shocked as I was by what was happening. What was going on?

What was going on was Kari's ten-year high school reunion! We had inadvertently walked into the exact location on the specific day and the precise time where Kari's high school reunion was scheduled to occur. What are the odds of that happening? Kari knew nothing about it; she had not received an invitation as she had been living on the east coast for several years. If I was speechless at what was happening, you should have seen the look on Kari's face. Stunned is probably the best word to describe it. Kari quickly decided to flee the building. "Let's get out of here," she said as she took my hand and led me through the crowd and out the front door. We were followed by the manager of the bar who set up a sign on the sidewalk that read "Private Party: No Entrance." If we had walked up to the pub five minutes later than we had, we wouldn't have been able to enter and would not have had that striking encounter. We would have passed right on by and not realized what we missed.

## A BIG BRIGHT LIGHT

At first blush, you might wonder why Kari was in such a hurry to leave. When I found out what was happening I wanted to stay, but that's because I'm a guy. I didn't remember all that went into getting ready for my ten-year high school reunion. As I thought back, I recalled getting the first invitation to my reunion months ahead of time. The preparation for that event began that day. There's a lot of taking stock and looking in the mirror that goes on when a reunion comes around. Dieting, exercising, new outfits, new hairstyles, you name it!

Not only that, but there is a certain amount of personal reflection that goes on. You think about the person you were in high school. You think about your classmates, and remember them as they were, and wonder what they are like now. Then you think about your own situation now, and how you have changed from the person you were ten years ago.

Attending an event like a high school reunion shines a big, bright light on your life. Many of your high school dreams died or changed. Some may have come true, but most are distant memories. That's why Kari was in such a hurry to leave. She had no time to prepare. She walked in on her reunion completely by surprise. The faces of her high school classmates were like a spotlight shining on her life. It was a light she'd just as soon avoid, especially without the time to get herself ready. I couldn't blame her. Could you? Would you want to look at your life under so bright a spotlight with no preparation?

All things being equal, we avoid that light. It just might be too much to take to think about all the ways that we have settled for less than our own highest ideals for our lives. But here is where a disciple of Jesus Christ must be different. We must not avoid the bright spotlight that shines on our lives, but we must seek out that light, and not every ten years! The spotlight I'm referring is the majestic light of God's holiness.

Throughout this chapter, I've been reflecting on the call to "Go and sin no more," the resolution to never sin again and the vocation to holiness and the perfection of charity. Making progress in the spiritual life is understood as growing in holiness. We grow in holiness as we strip and allow ourselves to be stripped of all that blocks and hides God's holiness from radiating in our lives. God's Holy Spirit lives in us. Our challenge is to live in a way that allows the Holy One to shine forth through our lives. Growing in holiness is not becoming more holy; it is more fully allowing Jesus Christ, who lives in us, to radiate and become manifest through us. As we strive over many years to "be holy in every aspect of our conduct" and to "be perfect as your heavenly Father is perfect," what happens? As the number of our sins decreases, and we find ourselves jumping less and less into sin, even as we continue to fall into sin, what shows up in our awareness? Do we find that we become more and more satisfied with our spiritual state, the more God's holiness shines through our lives? I ask the question because the answer will probably surprise you.

## THE GREATEST SINNER OR SAINT? YES!

The answer comes from the lives of saints, and is expressed in a very striking way by St. Paul in one of the latest writings that bears his name, 1 Timothy 1:15: *This saying is trustworthy and deserves full acceptance: Christ Jesus came into the world to save sinners. Of these I am the foremost.* Notice that St. Paul draws attention to two truths simultaneously: 1) Jesus Christ came to save sinners; and 2) he (St. Paul) is the worst sinner. At the end of his life, this amazing man who had undergone an incredible conversion, who desired only to live for the Lord Jesus and fulfill his God-given call to holiness and mission, considered himself the foremost sinner, the greatest sinner! He is saying that if you lined up all sinners, he would be at the front of the line. How are we to understand this statement?

In trying to interpret his meaning, we might conclude that he was using hyperbole, a literary device, where he exaggerates for the sake of effect. Others might say that St. Paul was making a statement that in his mind was objectively true. The horrible sins he committed before his conversion make him the worst sinner of all. I'm guessing a few might interpret this Scripture in psychological terms, concluding that St. Paul had an unhealthy, over inflated sense of his own sinfulness.

I'm not convinced that any of these three interpretations gets St. Paul's meaning. I propose that St. Paul's statement is an authentic, life-giving spiritual insight that each of us can have, and that each of us can say. How is that possible? If I am the worst sinner, that means that

Hitler was not, or someone whom we know to be doing truly evil things. How can more than one person be "the worst sinner"?

For each person to say "I am the worst sinner" is connected to growth in holiness, to drawing nearer to the infinitely Holy One Who is God. Remember the traditional idea behind living a confessional life? Our confession of faith is a simultaneous confession of God's glory and our sinfulness. As we grow in the perfection of charity, as we courageously resolve to never sin again, we become ever more profoundly aware of God's holiness. We come closer to Him in nearness and in likeness. As the light of God's holiness shines more deeply in our lives, it is *not* the case that our sense of our own sinfulness decreases. Rather, it increases. Hans Urs von Balthasar wrote about this dynamic in a text that I cannot locate, but it went something like this: in the lives of saints, as the number of their sins decreased, the horror over their sins that remained increased.

When St. Paul states that he is the worst sinner, he is making a confession of his own misery before God that shows up precisely through his deep union with God. The more intense and deep His sharing in God's holiness, the more convicted he becomes about his own lack of holiness. The imperfections that remain in him shine all that greater in his awareness. This is his perspective on himself, on his misery. What about how he sees the rest of us? He sees our sinfulness differently. Why? Because of the awareness in him of all the grace and mercy he has received from God despite the fact that he deserved the opposite. The bright light of God's holiness convicts him of his own infidelity, of all the times he's failed to recognize or respond to God's grace. What he doesn't know is how God's grace has been operative in other people's lives, so he has no way of judging anyone else's fidelity or infidelity. What he is convinced about could be stated in the following way: "I don't know what grace you've received, how you've been gifted by God or how God's grace has been operative in your life. What I do know is that God had been absolutely, completely faithful in offering His grace to me in my life, and what shows up in me is how unfaithful I have been...I cannot imagine how anyone could have done as poorly with what they've been given as I have done with what I've been given. I am the greatest sinner."

The holier that St. Paul becomes, the more his life displays the light of Christ. The more he is conformed to Christ, the greater the distance he realizes there is between the holiness of God and his miserable condition where he continues to sin. When we realize the holiness of God, we realize how pitiable and poor our own condition is before God. In God's light, we are not even tempted to glance over our shoulders at others, or to point our fingers at their failures; it's our own failures that are obvious and inexcusable. I am the worst sinner. Indeed.

WILL IT!

We are called to be saints, to be holy, to attain the perfection of charity. It is God's work of grace that chisels away all that blocks His holiness from shining in our lives. We are to be masterpieces of holiness. Without God's loving mercy, we would never be freed from the darkness that grips our lives. But what is our part to play in attaining the perfection of charity, of becoming a saint? During my time in the seminary, I heard told in a sermon a story about St. Thomas Aquinas. One day, a brother Dominican friar asked him the question, "What must I do to become a saint?" His response was only two words, "Will it." Is St. Thomas saying that becoming a saint is a matter of our own effort? No. Becoming a saint is not first of all or last of all associated with our effort. Rather, it is associated with God's gift and God's call for our lives. Our part is *to will* what *God wills for our lives.* What God wills for us is that we become saints, that we grow in holiness and attain the perfection of charity by loving Him with all our hearts, souls, minds and strength. We need to be able to say, "I will make it a priority, my first priority, to accomplish with my life what God's will is for me, that is, to be a saint."

When you think about all the things that you and I are determined to accomplish in our lives, all the things we make serious efforts to obtain, all the things we want to "grow" in, where does holiness fall on our lists? How much attention and intentional effort do we give to attaining the perfection of charity? How resolved are we to working on becoming a saint, and striving to live a life that honors God in every aspect of our conduct? The big challenge we face is not so much that we run from the call of God for our lives, but rather we crowd out the call to holiness because of all the other demands on our time, attention and energy. We just don't often feel a sense of urgency to be holy, as much as we are urgent about other matters.

Do you want to feel that sense of urgency to be holy? Do you want to strengthen your resolve to live a life that honors God in every aspect of your conduct? Go to Confession frequently. When we make our examination of conscience and are confronted by the light of God's truth, we will allow the deeper desires of our hearts, the desires that God planted there, to emerge in our awareness. We will discover in Confession the grace that heals our lives, lives that are unresolved or lacking in the resolve of seven-year old saints like Dominic Savio. We will be able to say with conviction, "I will never do it again." Why? Because I want to be a saint. I want to become the one God created me to be. I want to honor my heavenly Father and share His love more deeply. Nothing will get in my way. "Death but not sin" will be my motto. If we are striving for perfection, if we are striving to be saints, we need Confession. The regular practice of Confession will go a long way toward helping us realize that we are not yet perfect. Regular Confession will also help heal what is broken and strengthen what is weak so we can advance on the path of holiness. When it comes to Confession, practice makes perfect.

# PART III

# GO!

# CHAPTER EIGHT

# REALIZATION: PRACTICE MAKES PERFECT

*Have patience with all things,*
*But chiefly have patience with yourself.*
*Do not lose courage*
*in considering your own imperfections*
*but instantly set about remedying them.*
*Everyday begin the task anew.*

St. Francis de Sales

If you've made it this far into the book, I am hopeful you are ready and willing to go to Confession. However, I recognize that you may still have questions you want answered. As motivated as you might be by all of the positive reasons and benefits of going to Confession I laid out in earlier chapters, there may still be obstacles preventing you from taking a step into the confessional.

In this chapter, I answer the most commonly asked questions that sometimes stand in the way of someone going to Confession.

## DO I REALLY NEED TO GO TO CONFESSION REGULARLY, IF AT ALL?

If you are still asking this question, it is probably because you first opened the book to this chapter. I know so many Catholics who identify themselves as Catholic, who go to Mass faithfully and try to live in a way that honors God, but don't go to Confession regularly. They would never think about missing Mass on Sunday, but the idea that they should go to Confession more than once a year doesn't enter their minds, or if it does, it leaves quickly. Maybe that's you. Bottom line, why go to Confession, or at least, why go to Confession more than is strictly necessary? The answer is that sin is a disease and Confession is the cure Jesus Christ offers you. When you are sick, you take medicine. When you are really sick, you go see your doctor. Jesus Christ is your Divine Physician, the Confessional is His hospital and his "attending physician," the priest, is there to minister the treatment that will heal you spiritually and bring you all the other benefits listed in Chapter Five.

If you don't see yourself described in what I've just written, then please heed the words of a brief exchange found in a short story by G.K.Chesterton involving his famous priest detective Fr. Brown, and his then colleague, Flambeau: "'Can it cure the one spiritual disease?' asked Father Brown, with a serious curiosity. 'And what is the one spiritual disease?' asked Flambeau, smiling. 'Oh, thinking one is quite well,' said his friend."[1] If you don't see your need for Confession, please drive to your parish as if you are on the way to the Emergency Room. Your spiritual disease has advanced considerably. But a cure is still available. If you aren't moved by my analogy, then please go back and read this book from the beginning, and hopefully you will have greater insight into your condition and into God's desire to bring healing to your life through Confession.

## WHY DO WE HAVE TO CONFESS TO A PRIEST?

This is a very common question, not only from non-Catholics, but also from Catholics who have been away from the sacrament for a while. "Why can't I just ask God for forgiveness? God knows my heart. He knows that I'm sorry. He knows that I've been on my knees asking for forgiveness. Why isn't that sufficient?" We go to Confession to a priest because that is where Christ has promised to meet us with His healing mercy and forgive-

---

1. Chesterton, G. K., *The Complete Father Brown* (New York: Penguin Books, 1987), 132

ness. We should do the former without omitting the latter. You might appreciate this more clearly if we apply the same principle to the Mass and the Eucharist.

Do we commune with Christ by closing our doors and reading the account of the Last Supper in the Bible with our own bread and wine, or by attending Mass and receiving Holy Communion? The answer is that you commune in a sacramental manner with Christ at Mass because He has promised to meet you there. You may also have a type of spiritual communion with Him in your room as you read His Word. But understand clearly the radical difference between the two. In the second, my communing with Christ is my own spiritual action whereby I am seeking to remember what Jesus did at the Last Supper. At Mass, it is different. There, I am welcomed into the action of Jesus Christ Himself, and welcomed at His act of praise and thanks to the Father. When I commune with Jesus Christ at the place where He promises to meet me, in the sacraments, there is a radical difference in the effect it has on my life.

If we want to be forgiven by Jesus Christ for all the ways that we have dishonored Him through our sins, why wouldn't we honor Him by going to the place where He asks us to meet Him in order to be reconciled? It wasn't the Church's idea to establish confessing our sins to priests, it was Jesus' idea. Of course, He didn't establish confessionals. He didn't say, "I want you to build churches that have these rooms where you go and kneel and confess your sins through a screen or face-to-face." But He did say to His apostles, "'As the Father has sent me, so I send you.' And when he had said this, he breathed on them and said to them, 'Receive the holy Spirit. Whose sins you forgive are forgiven them, and whose sins you retain are retained.'" (John 20:21–23)

When He walked on this earth, Jesus manifested the Kingdom of God on earth through the forgiveness of sins. Not only that, but when He rose from the dead on Easter Sunday, He handed on to His apostles in the Upper Room that very mission to forgive sins, as seen in the quote above. How many times in the Scriptures is the forgiveness of sins part of what Christ does when He brings salvation to someone's life? He forgives sins to let the person know that God is reconciling the sinner to Himself. The scribes and Pharisees were always shocked by this, and the people were amazed. Why was this such a scandal? Because only God can forgive sins. Jesus was saying, "I Who am among you as a man am also 'God with you' Who has the right and authority to forgive your sins and bring you salvation."

When Jesus says to the apostles in the upper room, "If you forgive men's sins they are forgiven, if you hold them bound or retain them, they are retained," He is stating that the work of the apostles and their successors will involve extending the forgiveness of sins through their "ministry of reconciliation" which shows up today in Confession. Why confess to a priest? If you are really sorry, if you really want to ask God to forgive your sins, if you really are seeking a fresh start and a new beginning, then go to the place where you know Jesus Christ has promised to meet you with His forgiveness and healing. If you have a tumor that needs to be surgically removed you can't just call a surgeon on the phone, tell him about your problem, get some advice and then expect everything to be okay. You have to meet the surgeon at the hospital and let him cut you open and dig out the tumor, right? If you need medicine, you can't just call the doctor and say you need medicine. You have to go to his office, where he will examine you and give you a prescription for the medication you need. When we go to Confession, we meet Christ in the confessional where He performs spiritual surgery and prescribes the medicine we need to be healed.

## I HAVEN'T BEEN TO CONFESSION IN A LONG TIME. HOW CAN I FACE MY PARISH PRIEST?

While there are many Catholics who consider Confession a once-a-year duty, there are many others who haven't been in years, maybe even decades. Why haven't they gone in such a long time? There are four reasons I most often hear: 1) "I went to Confession growing up but one time had a bad experience;" 2) "I went to Confession occasionally growing up, but it was never really explained to me so I didn't get much out of it;" 3) "it was not emphasized in my upbringing—we rarely or never went to Confession as a family and/or we didn't hear or learn about it in my parish or Catholic school. When we did, it was often minimized in importance;" or 4) "all of my experience with Confession was done in communal settings. I haven't made an individual Confession since my First Reconciliation." Each of these four reasons ends with the phrase, "…and because of that I haven't been to Confession in years."

If one or more of those four statements is true for you, then my hope is that reading this book will motivate you sufficiently to want to go. But even if you are very motivated, that doesn't mean there still isn't a big hurdle standing in your way. For some of you, it is social embarrassment. "How can I go to Confession to Fr. Smith whom I see week after week, and confess to him that I haven't been to Confession in years (decades)?" There may even be a lingering fear or guilt about what Fr. Smith is going to say. Will he get upset, be disappointed or worse?

If you haven't been to Confession in many years, please read this clearly: if you showed up in Confession after being away for a long time, there are not twenty priests in the entire country who would get upset at you *in the confessional* for not going to Confession. I emphasize in the confessional because I wish more priests would preach more zealously *in the pulpit* about the gift of Confession and challenge Catholics to make a regular practice of going to Confession. Ideally, Fr. Smith would invite all his parishioners to come to Confession, and specifically address those in the assembly who have been away for years. Do not be afraid! Come and be reconciled, healed, forgiven and set free! It's such a life-giving message. Until that time comes, please believe me when I say almost every priest is going to be excited that you've decided to come back to Confession.

If you still find it particularly difficult to go to Confession to your pastor or parish priest, then please go to a nearby parish and go to a priest you don't know. If you want to make sure that the priest who will hear your Confession is not someone who will chastise you for how long you've been away, or chastise you for some other reason, then ask your Catholic friends which priest they go to for Confession. Once you get that first Confession off your chest, you may be willing to go to your own parish priest. Please know that priests do not want to be an obstacle to your going to Confession. I can't encourage you enough to find a priest who is not an obstacle to your going, and go!

## WHAT SHOULD I EXPECT WHEN I GO TO CONFESSION?

If it's been many years since you last went to Confession, you probably remember going into the church at the time scheduled for Confession, usually Saturday afternoon or before or after daily Mass, and standing in line along the wall or sitting in the pew waiting your turn before entering the confessional. Most confessionals had (and many still have) a central door where the priest sits, and a door or thick cloth on the right and left where you entered and knelt down on a kneeler in the dark, facing a small screen or grate. A door over the screen would slide open when it was your turn, and you would say your Confession through the screen.

Today, there are some Catholic churches where they still use the traditional confessional. However, many Catholic churches have replaced confessionals with what are often called reconciliation rooms. Upon entering, the first thing you usually see is a kneeler in front of a screen. Father will be sitting perpendicular to you behind the screen where he can't see you. You can kneel down and make your Confession through the screen, almost like whispering in the priest's ear. If you are comfortable going face-to-face, you just walk around the screen where you will find an empty chair facing the priest. You sit down and begin your Confession sitting in front of Father. Both ways of going to Confession are available in most parishes. If you want to make sure, just ask someone in the parish, or call the parish office and ask.

What is the best way to go to Confession, face-to-face or behind the screen? That depends on you. It will be determined by your personal history, the way you were formed in the faith, your personality and what you find comfortable. Some people who have been away for many years go anonymously for a time, and then switch over to going face-to-face. Catholics are drawn to different aspects of the sacrament. Those who want to focus on the aspect of confessing their sins and humbly expressing sorrow may be drawn to the traditional form which involves kneeling and speaking as central to the experience. Those who were brought up calling the sacrament Reconciliation may feel more drawn to sitting and confessing face-to-face. The key is for you to begin where you are and to do what you believe will help you get the most from the sacrament. That may not be the most comfortable for you, but the goal is encounter, not comfort. The crucified Lord intends to meet you and forgive you, so choose the manner of confessing that will best dispose you for that encounter.

I have one last note about the place where you confess. If you've been away from Confession for a long time and you feel comfortable with your parish priest, you might want to consider making an appointment to meet with him to make your Confession rather than confessing at scheduled times. Most parishes will indicate that Confession is at set times or by appointment. Consider making an appointment! Why would you do this? It will allow you time to confess without the pressure you might feel if you went during a scheduled time for Confessions. Your priest may appreciate this as well. I know that sounds radical to some. My dad spent many years away from the sacrament of Confession. When he finally went back, he decided he would go to his pastor, Father Joe Riley, who was a family friend. He could have gone somewhere else, another parish, where he could have received the sacrament anonymously, but he didn't. I remember two things about that Confession. The first was that my dad wanted to prepare well for his Confession. I helped him get ready. That was a special moment for me. In the days before his appointment, he wrote a list of what he wanted to confess so he wouldn't forget anything. The second memory I have is when my dad returned from his Confession. He said, "I feel so good! I feel like the weight of the world is off my shoulders." Maybe it's time for you to get freed of that weight.

## WHAT DO I SAY WHEN I FIRST GO INTO THE CONFESSIONAL?

A further block to going to Confession is not knowing what to say. I often hear, "How do I start? I forgot the prayers and don't remember what to do." If that describes you, my response to you is not to worry about figuring out exactly what to say in what order. The first thing to say is, "Father, I'm not sure exactly what to do because I haven't been to Confession in a long time. Please help me through this." If that happens, it's okay, but I would encourage you not to settle for that.

If you had a medical condition and you were going to see a doctor for it and you wanted to make sure you didn't forget anything, wouldn't it make sense to write down all the information and symptoms on a sheet of paper and take the sheet into the appointment with you? Don't be afraid to do what my dad did and write out a list of your sins. When I help my kids prepare for Confession, one of them finds it very helpful to write out her sins.

## WHAT'S GOING TO HAPPEN DURING THE CONFESSION?

When you enter the confessional or reconciliation room, the priest may welcome you with an invitation to make the sign of the cross or with a greeting, "Peace be with you." If invited to make the sign of the cross, please do that and then respond, "Amen." If addressed by the words "Peace be with you" respond by saying "And also with you."

At this point, the priest may read a passage of Scripture and share a few brief thoughts as a word of encouragement. If so, just be open to listen. Remember Jesus Christ is at work in this holy event. Be attentive to meeting Him in the Scripture, the prayers, the priest and in your heart.

At this point, it is customary to begin by saying "Bless me Father for I have sinned," or "Forgive me Father for I have sinned," and then follow with a statement about the length of time since your last Confession. "It's been such-

and-such number of weeks / months / years since my last Confession." It is then appropriate to confess your sins. For more help on the attributes of confessing well, please review Chapter Three in this book.

Once you've finished confessing your sins, the priest may ask for a clarification about something you've said, but will more often focus in on one or two things you've confessed and offer some counsel. He will end by naming a penance for you to do after Confession. If you don't understand what he is asking (e.g. you don't know how to say a prayer he asks you to pray), please don't be afraid to ask him a question. You will then be asked to make an act of contrition. At this point, it is customary to pray the *Act of Contrition*. (I included one traditional formulation in Chapter Four and most confessionals or reconciliation rooms include a copy of an *Act of Contrition*.) You may also be invited to express your contrition in your own words if you choose. I recommend, at least as you become accustomed to Confession again, that you pray a traditional *Act of Contrition*. When you finish your prayer, or maybe even while you are praying an *Act of Contrition*, the priest will grant you absolution by praying the following prayer with his hand extended towards you or by laying his hands on your head:

> God, the Father of mercies, through the death
> and resurrection of his Son has reconciled the
> world to himself and sent the Holy Spirit among us

for the forgiveness of sins; through the ministry of the Church may God give you pardon and peace, and I absolve you from your sins in the name of the Father, and of the Son, and of the Holy Spirit. Amen

After this, the priest will say some form of Dismissal to you, maybe in the form of a short prayer or through some other form such as, "Go in peace," to which you can reply, "Amen" or "Thank you Father."

## HOW DO I PREPARE FOR CONFESSION?

Throughout this book, I laid out the Catholic Church's teaching about the incredible benefits and amazing blessings that await you in Confession because Jesus Christ has promised to meet you there with His healing mercy and sanctifying grace. But a sacrament isn't magic. It requires something from you: the proper disposition or readiness to receive what Christ is prepared to give. The Catholic Church's spiritual tradition proposes two forms of preparation, both of which are part of preparing well for Confession. The two forms of preparation are called *remote preparation* and *proximate preparation*. Remote preparation has to do with the totality of your life of faith, how you were brought up and how you now live your faith. If you've read the book to this point, then you've figured out that the five sentences associated with Confession have roots in our everyday lives as disciples. This is what I mean by living a confessional life. Living a confessional life is your remote preparation for Confession. As you strive to live your life as a confession of faith, confessing God's glory and your misery, you are setting up your life for a fruitful Confession. Even more, if you embrace the five sentences that make up the heart of this book, you will be living a life that is inclined *towards* the Sacrament of Confession and flows *from* it. So, the long answer to your question about how to prepare for Confession is that your whole life as a disciple prepares you well for Confession. Or not.

There is also proximate preparation. Proximate preparation is the immediate preparation you make for Confession. What this means is that you should not just stumble into Confession, you should take time and effort to get yourself ready. Since most readers will be going to Confession on Saturday afternoon, I would propose that you should probably begin preparing much earlier that week. Make sure you set aside a personal prayer time on several consecutive days so that you can examine your conscience. If you are having a difficult time coming up with sins, pray the Penitential Psalms, or read from Part Three of the *Catechism* in the sections that cover the Ten Commandments. You can also use a shortened examination of conscience which you can find online or at your parish library or literature rack. If your parish doesn't have one, ask your parish priest for one. Don't forget to pray for true contrition for your sins. Remember that contrition, because it is rooted in love, is always a gift from God. Ask for that gift. Please refer back to Chapters Three through Five for many concrete examples and practical tips for what to confess and how to say it.

On the day of your Confession, please plan well. If you need babysitting support, set it up. If you need to bring your kids with you (as Kari or I have to do), make sure you arrive at the church prepared to go into the confessional. Otherwise, if your kids aren't as angelic as you need them to be, you may end up going into the confessional a bit flustered and unprepared. Don't get to the church ten minutes before Confessions are supposed to end. You might end up feeling like you have to go hastily, or the priest may need to hear your Confession more quickly than he would like. You want to arrive early enough to quiet yourself, slow down and turn to the Lord in prayer, asking for the grace of making a good Confession. Don't forget to bring your list of sins with you. Preparing well for Confession, both remote preparation and proximate preparation, are irreplaceable if you want to experience the healing power of this sacrament.

## HOW OFTEN SHOULD I GO TO CONFESSION?

I answered this question in Chapter Three but bring it up again here. How often? The answer is *regularly*. The challenge is to learn how to translate that answer into your life. Based on the teaching of the Catholic Church, and the words, exhortations and holy example of saints down through the millennia, the right answer is much more often than the typical practicing Catholic goes to Confession. Recommendations from priests and others I trust put the range between every two weeks and every two months. That might shock you. But consider again the benefits Christ has promised to pour out upon us in this sacrament and the necessity we have of that grace if we are to fulfill God's call for our lives. There is no way around it. Sick people need a doctor. People who have a regular recurrence of the spiritual disease of sin need to access the God-established remedy of Confession.

One factor that might impact how often you go to Confession is the degree to which you have integrated the five sentences mentioned in this book into your daily life. The more deeply you see your life as a disciple as a confessional life, the more that the grace of Confession is at work in your life before and after Confession. Though there's no hard and fast rule about how often we should go to Confession, if you're striving to live a confessional life, then going every two months will probably be sufficient because the essence of Confession is something you'll be living on a daily basis. The sacrament will play an important, even a critical role in giving you access to sacramental grace, but you'll also discover that living a confessional life is something that leads to Confession and flows from Confession.

## HOW WILL I FEEL AFTER CONFESSION?

Of course, the answer is, I don't know. I do know that the *Catechism* teaches, and my experience over many years confirms, that spiritual consolation is often experienced after Confession. This isn't just about being relieved, it's about being healed. If you don't feel anything, don't think you did something wrong. Don't try to manufacture a feeling. The true healing is spiritual and occurs at a depth that is beyond the senses, though God will often have the spiritual effect bubble up into our sense experience.

What is spiritual consolation like? I end this book with a story about my niece's First Reconciliation, which happened just two months before I completed this book. My sister told me the story about taking her young daughter Crystal to make her first Reconciliation. Crystal had some awareness and preparation for how to make a good Confession, but wasn't taught in any in-depth way about what to expect when she received absolution. After she made her Confession, she and her mom got in their car to drive home. It was then that Crystal said, "Mom after I went to Confession I just felt really light inside. I don't know how to explain it. It felt like there was this air inside me and it was just so light and it was really beautiful." This is what God has in store for you and me in

Confession. Spiritual consolation. Spiritual resurrection. Spiritual healing. We may not get the feeling, but we will have the effect, because it is based on Christ's promise to meet us and pour out His grace to us in the healing sacrament He established. He awaits you in the confessional. To meet you. To console you. To heal you. To set you free. Why would we run from that?

*The Mass: Four Encounters With Jesus*
*That Will Change Your Life*

"Dr. Curran's book not only lends itself to personal spiritual reading, but catechists and teachers can gain insight about how the leavening impact of the Eucharist can help those they serve draw closer to Jesus Christ. I heartily recommend this book."

Most reverend Joseph J. Tyson
Auxiliary Bishop, Archdiocese of Seattle

"As a long-time pastor, I highly recommend *The Mass: Four Encounters with Jesus that will Change Your Life.* With engaging illustrations, Dr. Tom Curran brings together his theological studies and his experience as the father of a growing family. [The book] will help young people understand the meaning of Mass and it will motivate all of us to make the Mass the 'source and summit' of our lives."

Fr. Phillip Bloom
Holy Family Parish, Seattle, WA

"This book addresses a very important pastoral reality, a crying pastoral wound in the Church, and that is, too many people find the Mass boring. The number one thing I like about this book is that it addresses in a successful way a real and vital issue—how do Catholics find Jesus at Mass. What could be more important to a Catholic than that?"

Fr. Kurt Nagle
Holy Family Parish, Kirkland, WA

"This wonderful book should be required reading in all Catholic high schools and RCIA programs. It presents a clear, thoughtful and lively invitation to deepen the way we encounter Jesus Christ at Mass."

Fr. Sean Raftis, S. J.

"The beauty of this book lies in [Dr. Curran's] simple, conversational approach—as if friends sat down over a cup of coffee to discuss the Mass...By unveiling the Mass as a real and personal experience, he helps to open our eyes, ears and hearts to this wonderful encounter with Christ."

Sue B.